hand of god

how god protects - popular notions realigned

govinda das

Tulsi
Books

Published and printed by:

Tulsi Books *(A division of Sri Tulsi Trust)*
7, K.M. Munshi Marg, Girgaum Chowpatty,
Mumbai - 400 007.
Web: www.tulsibooks.com

In association with:

Priyadarshini Academy
Email: priyadarshniacademy@gmail.com;
        pa@priyadarshniacademy.com
Tel: 022 22873456 / 66307160; Fax: 022 22022671
Web: www.priyadarshniacademy.com

First Print 2015 : 3000 copies
© 2015 TULSI BOOKS (A division of Sri Tulsi Trust)

ISBN:- 978-93-81283-29-5

OTHER BOOKS BY THE AUTHOR
- Voice Your Choice - Ethics from Epics Vol 1

COMING SOON
- Voice Your Choice - Ethics from Epics Vol 2
- Karna on Trial
- Women and Epics
- Science of Relationship - The Epic View

Write to author - queries108@gmail.com
Facebook.com/lessonsfrommahabharata

DEDICATION

To my guru, His Holiness Radhanath Swami Maharaja, whose love is the very foundation of my life and whose wisdom is the guiding principle of my actions.

To my param guru, H.D.G. A.C. Bhaktivedanta Swami Srila Prabhupada, whose belief system, dedication and faith has completely shaped my life.

To my parents, Sri Manu Naik and Srimati Laxmi Naik, to whom I owe the deepest values of my life.

To my friends from diverse backgrounds, whose wonderful lives have provided many invaluable insights and broadened the horizon of my understanding.

DEDICATION

To my guru, His Holiness Radhanath Swami Maharaja, whose love is the very foundation of my life and whose wisdom is the guiding principle of my actions.

To my param guru, H.D.G. A.C. Bhaktivedanta Swami Srila Prabhupada, whose belief system, leadership and faith has completely shaped my life.

To my parents, Sri Manu Malik and Smt. Neelam Malik, to whom I give the dearest values of my life.

To my friends from diverse backgrounds, whose wonderful lives have provided many invaluable insights and broadened the horizon of my understanding.

ACKNOWLEDGEMENTS

'Acknowledgement' as a term does not do justice to the sentiment in my heart. Hence I would rather like to express my gratitude to the numerous visible and invisible forces that have converged into making this book happen.

To name all of them here would be impossible. However, I would like to start with two of the most prominent teachers in my life: H.D.G. A.C.Bhaktivedanta Swami Srila Prabhupada, the founder of the Hare Krsna Movement and H.H. Radhanath Swami, author of the international best seller: The Journey Home – Autobiography of an American Swami.

I would also like to thank the two divine sages who have provided me countless inspiration, Valmiki Muni, the author of Ramayana and Maharishi Veda Vyasa, the author of the Mahabharata. My special thanks to the Gita Press edition of the Mahabharata. And to Prof. K.S.Narayanacharya, who deepened my appreciation and understanding of these scriptures.

My heartfelt gratitude to the team of transcribers who have made this book special - Anshuli Mathur, Vishal Sharma, Neeti Singh and Yogesh Singha.

I also take the opportunity to thank Amit Rohira for his overall efforts and to acknowledge the contribution of Ameya Tandel and Smruta Tandel for overall editing, proof reading and creative design.

And of course, my warm thanks to the entire team of Tulsi books and Priyadarshini Academy for making this book happen.

CONTENTS

PROLOGUE

On the material platform, any interaction with the objects of the senses - animate or inanimate, results only in repeated suffering. And despite our repeated endeavours, when we are unable to circumvent those sufferings, we approach God, with a hope of getting some relief from our perennial predicament or at least some momentary peace. Thus, one of the most amazing and innate phenomena of practicing spirituality is that it gives rise to expectations - like need for peace, desire for prosperity and happiness, etc.

It is observed that as one takes to spiritual practice (sadhana); a semblance of faith in God arises, bringing some peace of mind and general sense of well being. One even begins to enthusiastically advocate God's loving reciprocations and His power. However, with time, as some undesirable situations begin to surface and things don't look as hunky dory as they did in the initial stage of the spiritual journey, he begins to wonder. "Alas! Where is God now? How are things not going my way? Why is God not helping me?"

Often the practitioner is also consoled by others - "Just continue to have faith in Him and everything shall be alright". However the perfect material situations which he is always hopeful about never arrive. So he mechanically wades through his spiritual life, breeding scepticism about the overall situation, while pondering, "Has God become unresponsive? Is there anything wrong with my practice? What is going wrong?"

One might say - is this a natural course for all those who take up

i

to spirituality? If so, then how do we reconcile all this and still carry on with greater conviction in God?

The only way to reconcile this is that unless our faith is founded on conclusive truths of the scriptures, passed down through bona fide disciplic succession (guru-sisya-parampara), we run the risk of being mere sentimentalists under the name of spirituality. Such fanatical 'faith' only causes us harm and disrupts the lives of others.

Instead of endeavouring to help ourselves with the aid of scriptural knowledge, we become inert and lazy, thinking God will manage everything for us. Thus many simply become more and more weak, shaking the foundation of their pliable faith.

The concept of God's protection is very logically and reasonably explained in the scriptures. Real faith in sanatana dharma (eternal religion of the living entities), is based on proper knowledge of what faith really means and how the process of our surrender to God works. This entails understanding the intricacies of how karma, destiny, endeavour and time act on everyone.

Sri Krishna brilliantly illustrates to Arjuna, His dear friend and devotee, the concept of five factors behind every action (Bhagavad Gita, 18 Chapter, 14-15 verse). In other words, the five integrated factors that actually make things happen – the body (place of action), the performer (one who acts), the various senses (instruments of action), different endeavours (action itself) and the interception of supreme cause, or daiva.

Whatever right or wrong actions a man performs are caused by these five factors.

As spiritual aspirants and practitioners, what we fail to reconcile is that our part of endeavour should never be stopped. We have

ii

to identify the appropriate instruments and a favourable place where work can be carried out because endeavour is an essential part of our existence. If in spite of availability of instruments and place of action, we do not endeavour, then success is not possible.

Any lack of interest, absorption and alertness can lead to mishap. For instance, if a driver is not alert and conscious while driving, accident is the most probable outcome.

As explained above, when all the four immediate factors and the fifth, *daiva*, or hand of God, are working in tandem, then only our success or failure can be analyzed properly.

This is the theme of protection in its truest essence; the spiritualist does not become lazy or inactive; rather he collects all the right ingredients to act and depends on God, having done his duty and leaving the outcome to Him. He merely participates through his endeavours while God reciprocates unlimitedly.

If the foundational principle of how the hand of God works becomes distorted, then such a misconstrued conception leads to the individual endeavouring lesser and lesser while simply hoping that God will move the magic wand in making his life a success.

One village folk explained this equation about God's protection very simply. He said, "If you see technically, the living entity's effort is ninety-nine percent while God's grace is just one percent, but the actual impact of that effort on the outcome is just one percent and that of God's grace is ninety nine percent!" This is what the *Bhagavad Gita* precisely highlights.

Quantitatively speaking, to achieve success in life, we have to stake a lot by the virtue of our endeavours in comparison to God's grace. However, qualitatively the grace factor outweighs heaps of our endeavours.

To convey, inspire and assimilate this principle in our lives, I could not find anything more appropriate than the exemplary life and precept of the Pandavas, who were astutely faithful to Sri Krishna. They always gave more than hundred percent, and wherever they fell short, Sri Krishna duly compensated, more so to ensure the Pandavas' success and intensify their faith in Him.

I hope the readers internalise these concepts and lead a responsible and judicious life, wholeheartedly depositing their faith at Sri Krishna's lotus feet and His divine attributes.

INTRODUCTION

Protection entails dependence. Being independent implies that one does not need protection. When we accept authority i.e. seek protection, it indicates submissiveness in our attitude. Being protected gives rise to two emotions – a sense of assurance, and on the flip side, over-dependence, which occasionally leads to complacency. This creates a perpetual schism between the faithful and the faithless, a 'Tug of War' of sorts that is pushing and pulling the tangentially opposite belief systems of the believers and non-believers.

The faithful believe that God will protect, while the faithless say they have to seek their own protection. Both are antithetical and fixed in their own logic.

The faithless especially cannot understand how the principle of 'seeking protection' works for the faithful. The faithful, however, do not have such conflict as they are always aware how the hand of God wields its way in their lives which is inconceivable to the faithless.

What does it mean to be dependent on God? What does it mean to be faithful? All can be understood by a little glimpse into the lives of the Pandavas, who were ardent followers of *dharma*, or religion as given by God.

The non-believers, who have never experienced the hand of God are sceptical. They challenge - "How does God protect His followers or devotees? If indeed he does, then why do they face reverses in their lives? Consequently often those who are not devoted to God are also well situated. How is this possible?"

Critics vociferously speak about the sufferings meted out to the Pandavas. They retort, "What did the Pandavas gain after meticulously following *dharma*? They eventually struggled, lost their children and relatives in the fratricidal war, even killing their own brother Karna! So how was the outcome of their life any different from the Kurus' in regards to suffering? Kurus' suffered by dying and the Pandavas suffered while still alive!"

To reconcile all this is not so easy. Viewing it through the lens of mundane vision will only make us more perplexed. The lives of the Pandavas can be understood when one familiarises oneself with the foundational principles based on which the laws of this world affect individuals. For that, one needs to thoroughly imbibe the concept of God's incarnation in this world (*avatara*) especially as Sri Rama and Sri Krishna.

These *avataras* are typified by Their own unique conduct and philosophy. Actually the whole concept of how God protects and helps is very unique and must be viewed in the *dharmik* context. When we fail to decipher great epics such as *Mahabharata* and *Ramayana* through this lens, we misconstrue God's role in our life. This is one of the biggest ironies, for both believers and non-believers – having wrong expectations from God! Such fallacies raise doubts even in the believers, what to speak of reinforcing the scepticism of the non-believers.

Do such *avataras* forewarn their devotees about the problems they will encounter or how They will extend their protection? No. In fact, they don't even promise unceasing physical protection to their devotees. Rather, these *avataras* act inconspicuously, just to increase the struggle and self-endeavour of their devotees, making their hearts ever more grateful and prayerful.

Through the different stories of the Pandavas in this book, one will have a clearer picture of what real protection means.

The Pandavas exhibited three key principles when they took shelter of Lord Krishna's protection:

a) A grateful heart

b) A visionary mind

c) Action-oriented senses

Sri Krishna's protection brought forth these key principles in the lives of the Pandavas. The Pandavas were often in helpless situations yet they continued to act on the path of *dharma*, with hearts ever brimming with gratitude for Sri Krishna. We see from their impeccable and venturesome lives, how they always depended on Sri Krishna, especially in adversity, thus leading to unabated remembrance of the Lord.

Pandavas always remained self-sufficient, and the most essential aspect of which is to remain faithful backed by proper understanding. Their expectations were backed with efforts, applying appropriate strategy, correcting wrong moves, and learning to evolve by making changes, acting on those changes, collecting the right resources, experiencing setbacks, always remaining united in chaos and conflict, within and without, and seeking guidance from Kunti, Vidura, Draupadi and a host of sages, and of course, the foremost of all - Sri Krishna, who was protecting them in a very unique way.

This book attempts to evince what the hand of God entails for each one of us and to get an inkling of what to expect through the precept of the Pandavas' life and how to channelize our life's endeavours.

chapter I
DHARMAVEER DESCENDS

About 5,500 years back, when the entire earth, formerly known as Bharat Varsha was overburdened by the rule of unscrupulous and exploitative kings inflicting severe atrocities, Dharmaveer Sri Krishna descended to this world.

After the marriage ceremony of Vasudeva and Devaki, as is customary, Devaki was to leave for her husband's home and due to imminent separation from her; all her relatives were in great agony. Among them was her cousin Kamsa, the ruler of Mathura, who out of deep affection for her, personally took the reins of the chariot to ride his newly-wed sister and brother-in-law to their home. But en route, frightened upon hearing a prophecy about the eight child of Devaki being the cause of his death, Kamsa's mood suddenly transformed, and he decided to kill his sister on the spot. Instead of the reins and the whip, he now held the soft silken hairs of Devaki in one hand and a deadly upraised sword in the other.

To save his wife, Vasudeva, who was an expert diplomat, promised Kamsa that he would deliver to him all the children born of her, thus ensuring Kamsa's safety, as Devaki was not a threat for Kamsa per se. Being aware of Vasudeva's integrity, Kamsa instantly relented and allowed them to proceed.

As promised, Vasudeva presented his first newborn child to Kamsa, who, being amazed by his magnanimity allowed Vasudeva to take it back. However, being provoked and convinced by Narada Muni, that irrespective of the order of birth, any child could be the eighth, the infuriated Kamsa immediately shackled both Devaki and Vasudeva and threw them in the dungeon of his prison and brutally killed six of their new-born sons, one after another by smashing them against a rock. The seventh child was transferred to the womb of Vasudeva's other wife, Rohini, and Devaki was rumoured to have had a miscarriage.

Kamsa was now waiting for the eighth child in great anxiety. Sri Krishna appeared from Devaki's womb in His transcendental four-armed Vishnu form, but on Devaki's prayers transformed Himself to appear like an ordinary new-born baby with two hands. Devakinandana then inspired Vasudeva to take him to Gokula to the house of Nanda Maharaja without letting Kamsa know about His birth. Thus, Vasudeva, one who was known for his impeccable integrity and word of honour, broke the promise he had made to Kamsa.

Thus we see that from the beginning, Mukunda put His devotees to test. What is pertinent - the word of honour or the purpose of the promise?

It was not easy for Vasudeva to forsake his word to Kamsa in order to protect the child as it could mean blemishing his hitherto flawless character. But, knowing the purpose of his action, he willingly did it for the betterment of the entire suffering humanity as well as himself.

This is a very important principle of *dharma* - to discern the difference between the letter of the law, and justice. The essence of law is to provide justice, but sometimes the very same law unfortunately becomes an instrument of gross injustice. Only the truly honest and altruistic, those who can see through reality holistically, sometimes break the law, not out of weakness, but for the highest welfare of all involved, thus establishing the true purpose of law – to provide justice.

2

Vasudeva took Devakinandana across the river Yamuna, placed Him in the house of Nanda and Yashoda, and brought their child back to Kamsa's prison. Being informed of the birth of the eighth child and completely unaware of what had actually transpired through the night due to divine will, Kamsa hastily rushed to kill the baby girl, even though Devaki repeatedly pleaded him not to. Unrelenting, he tried to strike the baby, but she slipped from his hands and flew in the sky, making a prophecy of his imminent punishment and disappeared.

Kamsa then devised many schemes to kill Shyamsundar but failed every single time, not realizing that he was trying to achieve the impossible. He sent many demons to Vrindavana, and each of them became the object of Nandalal's sport and a means of entertainment for His cowherd friends. In the process, all the demons were liberated by awarding them death.

As Kanhaiya was growing up with his elder brother Baladeva, one fateful day, Srila Narada Muni, the spiritual master of Srila Vyasadeva, arrived in Sri Vrindavana *dhama* after having visited Kamsa. Narada Muni had revealed the secrets about Sri Krishna & Lord Balarama to Kamsa.

Just after Keshidamana had killed the Keshi demon, disguised as a horse, Narada Muni approached Him, describing how he would witness His upcoming pastimes; the ones He would perform after leaving Vrindavana. He narrated how Kamsara would kill Kamsa after killing Chanura & Mushtika and eventually marry Rukmini & Satyabhama. He also foretold how Dwarkadhish would kill Shishupala, the king of Chedi, in the *Rajasuya yagya* conducted by Yudhisthira Maharaja. Narada Muni further mentioned how Parthasarathi would accept the role of Arjuna's charioteer & become instrumental in removing the burden of all the demoniac forces in the garb of Kings on Mother Earth.

Meanwhile the Pandavas were growing up, almost as contemporaries of Damodara, but having had no personal encounters with Him yet. Certainly they had heard about Him from Mother Kunti, who was His aunt, however they had not yet directly encountered Shyamsundar nor experienced His personal support. After their father's sudden loss, when they came back to Hastinapura, the Kurus, headed by Duryodhana, ill-treated them. Duryodhana even tried poisoning Bhima, but he miraculously survived and in fact thrived, even in this dangerous plot.

The Pandavas were incessantly inflicted with challenges and adversities. But this does not mean they were bereft of Bhaktavatsala's protection. In fact, God ensures that we experience diversities and dualities in our life and it is all pre-arranged in our journey towards Him. The Pandavas' life was full of challenges, but they were grateful for this, because this made them strong, agile, experienced, and of course, ultimately feel the inconspicuous hand of God.

They were inherently connected with the Supreme Personality of Godhead, Sri Krishna, through their upholding of religious principles even in the most testing times. This shone forth through their virtuous discipline, model cooperation, relentless dedication, exemplary service to their spiritual teacher and respect to all superiors, including Dhritarashtra. They even tried their best to cooperate with their cousins, headed by Duryodhana. Certainly these qualities are universally laudable. Thus, the Pandavas exemplified the fact that Lord favours those who are deserving of His mercy and attention.

Interestingly, while in Mathura, few days after having destroyed King Kamsa, Devakinandana had sent Akrura to Hastinapura as a messenger! What was the content of that message? It conveyed how Dhritarashtra was supposed to take care of the Pandavas.

Amogha Krishna warned Dhritarashtra of the consequences of not treating the Pandavas properly. And as is seen from the *Mahabharata*, Dwarkadhish orchestrated everything to ensure the Pandavas emerge victorious in the end.

But it would be rather abnormal to the nature of this world if a supposed follower of God was to be pampered by not being exposed to any sorrow or distress; Dinanatha is not like a pampering father, who provides all kinds of indulgences to His child. How can growth be experienced in such an environment? And what good can such a pampered individual, bereft of existential knowledge do to others? One who is always protected physically can never experience life's realities. He or she would be in an artificially controlled environment and never exposed to the practical side of life. So what is the point of such treatment?

chapter 2

STRUGGLE, STRATEGY & SUCCESS

Soon after Akrura returned to Mathura, conveying Yadunandana's message to Dhritarashtra, Duryodhana and his party coaxed him to send the Pandavas to Varnavata for a vacation. They intended to kill the Pandavas by burning their palace, which was strategically built using inflammable materials. Vidura, with his keen observation and sharpness, sensed this plot, and instantly warned the Pandavas. He provided them with the facility to dig a tunnel to help them escape whenever the imminent fire breaks out.

In fact, a day before Duryodhana had actually planned their massacre; the Pandavas ignited the house themselves and escaped through the tunnel. They stayed incognito for a while, ensuring that the rumour of their death spreads. Given the eventuality of continued onslaught from the wicked Duryodhana and his party, it was strategically the best means to save themselves for the time being. When the news broke, Sri Krishna externally mourned for the death of the Pandavas, but in reality He was aware of their whereabouts.

In the forest, they roamed like nomads, donning different disguises. Although of diverse natures, Mother Kunti's love, which was their greatest wealth, kept them united through trying times. As they wandered from place to place, they were once attacked by Hidimba, a man-eating demon. A fight ensued and Bhima emerged victorious, killing the demon with great force, thinking as if he were punishing Duryodhana. Bhima's hands were tied as he could not punish the tyrannical Duryodhana for his repeated attempts to mistreat and even finish them and now he was releasing that pent up anger on Hidimba. His sister Hidimbi fell in love with Bhima and begged Kunti's blessings to marry her heroic son. Although Bhima was shy and unwilling as his elder brother Yudhisthira had still not married, Kunti, overlooking the general rule gave her loving consent for the marriage.

Thereafter, following a long course of travel, the Pandavas reached Kampilya, the capital city of Maharaja Drupada. When Drupada Maharaja was attacked by the Kurus, at the behest of Dronacharya, Drupada had taken two vows - to have a daughter who would marry Arjuna as he held Arjuna in the highest regard, and to have a son who would kill Dronacharya; both of whom were eventually born of a fire sacrifice.

Upon hearing of the death of the Pandavas in Varnavata, Drupada was disheartened but one of his *purohitas* (family priest) pointed out that pious souls like the Pandavas could not succumb to an accidental death. He suggested that if the king were to declare Draupadi's *svayamvara* (an ancient Indian practice of choosing a husband from among a list of suitors), the Pandavas would certainly appear. This prophecy came to pass! They arrived in time for the *svayamvara*.

The ceremony, led by the Lord of the Pandavas, Sri Krishna and Balarama, was attended by many stalwart kings vying to win Draupadi's hand. Sri Krishna recognized the Pandavas, whose bodies, though covered by dirt, were just like fire covered by smoke, and He informed Balarama of their presence. However, the other assembled kings, distracted by the thought of winning Draupadi's hand in marriage, did not notice the Pandavas.

The one, who could successfully shoot an arrow at the eye of a revolving fish while looking at its reflection in the water below, would marry Draupadi. Many great kings and princes tried their fortune but failed. And when Karna came forward, Draupadi clearly expressed her decision not to marry Karna, him being the charioteer's son. This, in one sense, distracted Karna and even he missed the target.

Among all the assembled suitors who were unsuccessful at performing this feat, only Arjuna was actually capable of accepting such a challenge. This feat demanded intense concentration, acute sense of timing and great precision. The greatest archer Arjuna then walked up to the arena, went close to the bow, standing there like a mountain, and then circumambulated it. He offered obeisances to Shiva, the Lord of destruction, and in his mind offered obeisances and lovingly remembered his most intimate friend Sri Krishna. Thus Arjuna's consciousness of Shyamsundar was ignited. He felt a strong sense of His presence in the assembly. With this mood, he lifted the bow.

It is evident that Kunti had inundated the Pandavas with narrations about the greatness of Giridhari, resulting in Arjuna's spontaneous consciousness of Him, within and without.

As Arjuna picked up the bow and successfully pierced the target, the eye of an artificial fish, it caused uproar in the assembly. The *brahmanas* retaliated by throwing their upper cloth, while the assembled kings were shocked and dismayed to see an anonymous archer victorious. Although the victor had the gait of a lion-like warrior, externally he appeared just like a *brahmana*. The other humiliated kings tried to attack Drupada, but the Pandavas, exhibiting their prowess deftly defeated each one of them.

Of course, such a remarkable battle lead by His dear Pandavas, Arjuna & Bhima could not have skipped Sri Krishna's attention. He told His brother, "O Balarama! The one with the gait of a lion, playfully carrying a bow the size of a Taal tree, is certainly Arjuna! Be assured. If I am Vasudeva, My words cannot be false. And

chapter 3
DRAUPADI ORDAINED BY DESTINY

After winning Draupadi's hand, the Pandavas returned to the house of the potter, where they were residing, on the outskirts of Kampilya. Upon arriving, they told Kuntidevi, "Mother, look what we have got as *bhiksha* (charity received by begging)." Kuntidevi, without looking, replied from inside the hut, "Share it equally among yourselves." But when she realized that the *bhiksha* was actually a bride won by Arjuna, she became extremely unhappy at what she had spoken, though her words were actually meant to fulfill a prophecy pertaining to Draupadi's destiny. According to Lord Shiva's benediction, she was to marry five men. Srila Vyasadeva told the Pandavas about this as they were proceeding to their marriage ceremony, clearly spelling out that they were destined to marry her, and she was destined to marry them. He explained how it was ordained by the higher power and was thus sacrosanct.

It is interesting, how Vyasadeva is one character in the Mahabharata, who on some occasions foretells certain future incidents, to alert and prepare the Pandavas about some extraordinary events. This concept shall be discussed later on.

When confusion prevailed over who would marry first, Arjuna told Yudhisthira that he could not commit the *adharma* of marrying Draupadi unless Yudhisthira and Bhima had first tied the knot. As they were discussing this, Yudhisthira Maharaja realized that in order to unite all his brothers for the cause of *dharma*, they all had to marry Draupadi. Then Yudhisthira Maharaja made a very pertinent point, that since the thought of all the five brothers marrying Draupadi had already occurred to him, it couldn't be *adharmik* because being *Dharmaraja*, the personification of *dharma* himself, nothing but *dharma* could enter his mind. And Srila Vyasadeva had already asserted this fact.

All of a sudden, Sri Krishna along with Balarama appeared at their place heralding Their supreme approval and blessing upon this decision. Thus, the verdict was not only approved by Vyasadeva, the compiler of the *Vedas* and *Dharmaraja* Yudhisthira, the personification of discipline, but also by Sri Krishna Himself, the original establisher of *dharma* and the original compiler of *Vedas* and the conclusion of the *Vedanta*. Devakinandana appeared at the time of making the decision and expressed His pleasure about the final verdict.

Since this was the first official interaction between the Lord and His dear Pandavas, the Lord took the liberty of introducing Himself to them, beginning with Yudhisthira Maharaja. He said, "It's Me, Krishna" and promptly touched his feet. Balarama also came forward and offered His obeisance to Yudhisthira Maharaja. Then both the brothers, Krishna and Balarama, touched the feet of Pandavas' mother, Kuntidevi. Yudhisthira Maharaja asked Krishna, "My dear Vasudeva, when we came to the assembly of King Drupada, we were disguised. Then how did You recognize us?" He smilingly replied, "My dear Yudhisthira, how much ever the fire tries to hide itself, it cannot. How is it possible for anyone other than the Pandavas to perform such a wonderful feat of winning the contest organized by Maharaja Drupada? It's our good fortune that you have become victorious and that you were unharmed by that great fire in the Varnavata. The conspiracy of Dhritarashtra, along with his sons and ministers did not harm you at all; this is our good fortune. Whatever is destined will surely come to pass. You are like the incessant fire. You will continue to grow." After speaking thus, Keshava said, "My dear Yudhisthira, now We should depart from this place, so that the

12

other kings don't recognize you." Taking permission thus, along with Balarama, He walked out of the place of the fortunate pot seller, in whose house the Pandavas were residing.

This incident reveals how Madhava's concern for the Pandavas was beyond the realm of physical proximity. The Pandavas were given a special place in His heart, and hence in His blessings and good wishes. He also foretold the Pandavas that they were destined to be like an ever-increasing fire, which no power in this world could extinguish.

The marriage of the Pandavas with Draupadi is most intriguing and bewildering, even to the soberest of minds. It has caused great perplexity even for scholars with firm intelligence, who are otherwise adept at reconciling most complex doubts and conflicts found in the scriptures. This kind of marriage was unprecedented, and will never be repeated any time in the future. No one can imitate this, nor is any one capable of handling such situations.

To view this marriage from a mundane perspective will only cause commotion; therefore it has to be seen from a higher dimension. Vyasadeva represents the subtle workings of the higher realities. He represents the concept of *daiva* (providence) - that which is unchangeable. No force in the world can change or direct destiny elsewhere. So when the great sage Vyasadeva foretold such a sacrosanct event, the best possible means was to submit to it, knowing that it was coming from a transcendental realm.

It was the greatness of the Pandavas who accepted this most unwarranted and unprecedented fate and lived through it for the rest of their lives with utmost dignity and honour. It was neither coincidence, nor abrupt, nor was it just to honour the words of Kunti. She was simply an instrument of *daiva*, as indicated by Vyasadeva.

After their marriage, Draupadi became the very purpose of their life. She was like their very soul and they were like the five *pranas* (life-force). When the soul dwells in the body, it sustains and survives on these five *pranas*.

After Draupadi's arrival in the lives of the Pandavas, Kunti played only a support role, appearing when essentially necessary. Draupadi became their centric force, their dignity and their cause for establishing *dharma*. She was Sri Krishna's greatest friend and He used her as the most powerful instrument in bringing all the unscrupulous people together and relieving the burden of the earth by eliminating them. In fact she was the final instrument in bringing out *adharma*.

Yadunatha protected the Pandavas by bringing Draupadi in their lives and stirring their life making it action-packed. It was not easy but it was surely fulfilling as they waded their way forward, learning through setbacks and reflecting, being at the feet of great sages and *rishis*.

chapter 4
KHANDAVAPRASTHA
TO INDRAPRASTHA

After the Pandavas' marriage to Draupadi, etiquette demanded that Dhritarashtra send them an invitation. Bhishmadeva decided to get them back to Hastinapura and Vidura was sent to escort them. This very much ached the hearts of Duryodhana and his brothers, as they realized that on the Pandavas' return to Hastinapura, they would have to part with the usurped kingdom they were enjoying, although Duryodhana was not the rightful heir to the throne. But they had to accede to the will of their superiors.

Although the Pandavas, headed by Yudhisthira Maharaja were the rightful heirs to sovereignty, but in order to buy time and avoid conflict, the Kurus decided to divide the kingdom. In fact, for all the evil that Duryodhana had inflicted upon the Pandavas, he was to suffer his due legitimately, but instead, the elders, turning a blind eye, tried by ostensibly just means to divide the indivisible kingdom.

The elderly Kurus divided the kingdom into two parts, which was actually unconstitutional, since it was not their personal property. No one can rightfully divide a kingdom, causing emotional rupture between the citizens of one part and the other.

Thus, Hastinapura was made one part of the kingdom to be ruled by Dhritarashtra with Duryodhana as prince regent. And Khandavaprastha, the other part, was awarded to Yudhisthira Maharaja. This place was earlier ruled by Pururava, Ayu and Nahusha, however because of some conflict with the *rishis*, the entire Khandavaprastha had now become a dense forest.

Purushottama was agreeable with the decision of the Kurus. He explained to the Pandavas that this was an amiable outcome, which would increase their fame and so they should act on it promptly. On being advised thus, the Pandavas decided to move to Khandavaprastha without delay. On arriving there, they discovered it to be a formidable dense forest. But by the grace of Purushottama Sri Krishna, the Pandavas eventually converted it into an abode of exquisite affluence. As the Lord entered into the forest, He instantly remembered Indra, who, realizing that Krishna was remembering him, immediately summoned Vishwakarma.

Offering his obeisances to Madhusudana, Vishwakarma submitted, "O Lord, please order me as You desire." In response, He directed him to build an enchantingly beautiful city there. He proclaimed that this magnificent city would be named after Indra as 'Indraprastha' and not Khandavaprastha anymore. The Pandavas then performed the ground-breaking ceremony and Vishwakarma, in no time, built a masterpiece, which became acclaimed world-wide. The ordinary forest was now transformed into a beautiful garden. Eventually the Pandavas performed the house warming ceremony, with Madhusudana at the center. As the process of ceremoniously entering into the city was completed, Sri Krishna decided to return to Dwarka.

Yudhisthira Maharaja, seeing Him ready to depart, expressed, "O Vrishninandana! It is only because of Your grace that we have received our kingdom. This forest transforming into a beautiful city is nothing but the fruit of Your mercy and this sovereignty is the result of Your compassion on us. O Krishna! O Madhava! You are our supreme goal – past, present and future. You are our all in all – our father, mother and our *Ishtadeva* (worshipable Lord). We do not know who Pandu is, we only know You. O Krishna! Please engage us in

16

whatever way You think is befitting. Just order us and we shall execute it".

Govinda responded, "O greatly fortunate Yudhisthira, by your own influence alone have you achieved this kingship, which is non-different from *dharma*. This kingdom belongs to your ancestors. It was impossible that you would be kept bereft of it! The sons of Dhritarashtra are evil-minded but what bad can they do unto the Pandavas? You continue to perform your duty as a king and follow the *dharmik* principles diligently. Keep serving great saintly *brahmanas* and very soon Sri Narada Muni will appear in your palace. Carefully listen to every word he speaks and heed his instructions conscientiously."

For the first time, Sri Krishna directly involved Himself in the nitty-gritty of the Pandavas' move from Hastinapura to Khandavaprastha. He suggested that they accept the proposal of moving their base to another place as it would aid further expansion. The Lord Himself planted the seed of that growth by personally ordering Indra and the engineer of the demigods, Vishwakarma, to build the city of Khandavaprastha. His logic behind the move was very simple – expansion is easier in an independent facility. When many stake-holders with multiple viewpoints are involved in expansion, individual roles get diluted leading to waning interest and enthusiasm.

Sri Krishna observed that the Pandavas were in a way, left high and dry by the decision-making elders in the Kuru dynasty, but He used this to their advantage. They built the capital city exactly suited to their requirements, which was only possible without the interference of inept elders.

Due to this autonomy, the Pandavas could strategically expand without having to conduct the formality of seeking permission from the elders. Of course that is not to say they wouldn't seek their blessings. The Pandavas became independent but not reckless. They used their sovereignty for boundless expansion.

Sri Krishna then visited His aunt Kuntidevi. He offered obeisances to her and requested her blessings to proceed on His journey. Kuntidevi said feelingly, "O Keshava! Whatever difficulties I have endured in Lakshagriha are unfathomable even to my father Kuntibhoja. O Govinda! Only because of Your support have I been able to cross the insurmountable ocean of misery. O Prabhu! You are the friend of the fatherless, and especially of the weak. Just Your *darshan* eradicates all our miseries. Please do remember the Pandavas at all times. Their very life can be sustained only by Your good wishes." On hearing the genuine, heartfelt plea of Kunti, Dwarkadhish responded, "Certainly My dear mother, I will follow your order." Offering her obeisances again, He then proceeded along with His brother Balarama, constantly thinking of Dwarka.

As predicted by Sri Krishna, Narada Muni visited the Pandavas. Since all five Pandavas had the same wife, there was a risk of conflict arising amongst them. Sri Narada intuited this, pointing it out and explaining a likelihood of misunderstanding looming ahead of them. To further illustrate, he narrated the story of the great demons Sunda and Upasunda. They had nice fraternal bonding, but discorded with each other on the issue of marrying Tilottama, a beautiful *apsara* created by Lord Brahma. Narada Muni therefore enjoined the Pandavas to have a stipulated decorum concerning their relationship with Draupadi. He said, part of that protocol should be that when one of the brothers was in her company, the other four would not interfere and if they did so, they would be banished to the forest for twelve years.

18

chapter 5

12 YEAR EXILE FOR ARJUNA

One day, while Yudhisthira Maharaja was with Draupadi, one *brahmana* impetuously approached the Pandavas relating that his cows were stolen. Indicating that if they were not retrieved, his religious sacrifices would stop and his family life would be disrupted as both his *dharma* and *artha* would be ultimately destroyed, he begged Arjuna to get his cows back.

This put Arjuna in a dilemma because his weapons were stored inside the quarters where Draupadi was in the company of Yudhisthira Maharaja and he couldn't have tackled those thieves without them. Arjuna was aware that by the stipulated decorum he could not intrude their privacy. He contemplated, "If, by breaking this rule, I am despised by my brother, I would not mind. And if I die by going to the forest, it doesn't matter, because protection of cows and *brahminical* culture is the topmost *dharma* and I must perform it at any cost."

This is the resolve of the Pandavas in regards to protection of *yagya* and knowledge. Cow protection leads to prosperity and protecting bona fide *brahmanas* means protection of wisdom. Thus Arjuna was willing to forgo the pleasure of newly-built Indraprastha and his dear wife Draupadi, to ensure protection of the *brahmana's* cows. Actually Arjuna was not in a dilemma but was rather making a resolve. By this, he endorsed Sri Krishna's opinion that the kingdom of the Pandavas was verily *dharma*.

Resolving thus, Arjuna entered Yudhisthira's quarters, grabbed his weapons, chased the robbers, protected the cows, fulfilled his duty to the *brahmana* and eventually decided to head to the forest for twelve years. Being informed of the exigency behind Arjuna's untimely entry into his quarters, Yudhisthira Maharaja pleaded him not to execute the vow as his actions were contingent. Moreover, as a younger brother, Arjuna had the leeway to enter his quarters, without it being considered a sin. But Arjuna asserted that rules were sacrosanct and that he must proceed to the forest.

This is the extent to which the Pandavas sacrificed to uphold *dharma*. They did not expect miracles in their lives; rather, they acted discerningly and took the responsibility. This was a distinct way in which Dinabandhu protected the Pandavas. He protected their *dharma*, their judiciousness, their truthfulness, and their vows, and gave them the confidence to follow their path.

Thus the resolute Arjuna decided to move out of Indraprashtha for twelve years. He was eager to practice *dharma* and embellish his learnings through his travels. He travelled with many enlightened *brahmanas*.

When he reached Gangadwara, he met Ulupi, the daughter of Naga. Ulupi begged Arjuna to marry her, saying that she would die in separation from him otherwise. Arjuna told her about the vow. Ulupi was aware of his vow and assured him that marrying her was no transgression as the vow was in relation to Draupadi. Arjuna, convinced that he was not straying from *dharma*, thus married her. Through her, he begot Irvan, who fought valiantly during the battle of Kurukshetra and died a heroic death.

Next Arjuna came to Manipura, north-east of Bharat Varsha and met Chitragandha, the daughter of Chitravahana. Arjuna married her too and stayed there for three years, before continuing his journey. When a little over a year was left in his exile, he arrived at Prabhasa *kshetra*.

Keshava was informed by His spies of Arjuna's whereabouts and decided to meet with him. Upon meeting, they embraced lovingly and enquired about each other's welfare. Sri Krishna was curious to know about Arjuna's travels and his activities in different *tirthas* and Arjuna joyfully recounted his adventures to Him. In this way, the great Nara and Narayana *rishis* relished each other's association.

Although Arjuna's exile was an outcome of his apparent infringement of decorum, it served as a great cause to form allegiances on behalf of the Pandavas with many great kings. In fact, the Pandavas were always on the move, whether by choice or by providence. Nevertheless, through these travels, they made friends, formed alliances and grew wiser.

They proved the old adage that any kingly order that settles down perishes. This was evident from the lives of the Kurus who had settled and become conditioned to relaxation and enjoyment, but the Pandavas were constantly on the move. Hrishikesh thus aided the Pandavas' growth by making them learn life's lessons, see the diversities in their mobile environment and experience dualities such as life and death, victory and defeat, comfort and distress, royalty and insignificance, community and life of solitude. These aspects cannot be realized theoretically. The Pandavas practically encountered and experienced them in their lives.

These experiences enhanced Arjuna's maturity and his relationships grew richer. And all this was maneuvered under the watchful eyes of Hrishikesh.

chapter 6

SUBHADRA'S ADVENTUROUS MARRIAGE

During this period, the great brother of Shyamsundar, Sri Balarama was negotiating the marriage of His sister Subhadra with Duryodhana, which neither Vasudeva and Devaki nor Shyamsundar were in agreement with. Thus Nandakumar decided to trick Balarama. This portion of the story has been explained in *Srimad Bhagavatam.*

Devakinandana decided to play a prank on His very own brother Balarama so as to protect Subhadra by stopping her marriage with Duryodhana and to strengthen the Pandavas' alliance with the Yadavas.

Earlier, on seeing Subhadra, Arjuna had felt immense attraction, thus he seeked permission from Yudhisthira to abduct her, which he willingly consented to. The act of a great *kshatriya* like Arjuna abducting a *kshatriya* princess was not necessarily irreligious; rather it was an exhibition of valour, as was customary then, among the royal order.

This move was also backed by superiors like Krishna and Yudhisthira, more so because it would protect Subhadra, who would otherwise be at the mercy of the evil-minded Duryodhana. Yadunatha thus suggested that Arjuna come to Dwarka in the guise of a *sannyasi* (a monk in the renounced order).

Arjuna, disguised as a *sannyasi*, stayed in the house of Vasudeva and Devaki, in anticipation of the right time to abduct Subhadra. At the opportune moment, Arjuna abducted Subhadra using a chariot given by Dwarkadhish. When the soldiers informed Balarama that the abductor was actually Arjuna impersonated as a *sannyasi*, He was infuriated. Balarama saw this act of Arjuna as audacious, arrogant and replete with hypocrisy. Balarama told Sri Krishna that it was as insulting as Arjuna putting his foot on His head and that a punishment for Arjuna was in order.

All the Yadu Kumaras were in support of Balarama's decision. But Yadunatha exhorted, "My dear Brother, it is indeed our good fortune that an illustrious person such as Arjuna would be Subhadra's bridegroom. He is such an accomplished *kshatriya* and our sister is a fit princess. She will be fortunate to have a husband like Arjuna, who is invincible. So, instead of retaliating, if You request Arjuna to return to Dwarka along with Subhadra, then We can arrange for a majestic wedding."

On hearing Devakinandana, Balarama's mind transformed and He consented. Arjuna and Subhadra were brought back to Dwarka and ceremoniously wedded. Arjuna stayed in Dwarka for some time and soon, Subhadra gave birth to their glorious son Abhimanyu.

Eventually, on the completion of Arjuna's twelve years of exile, he approached Indraprastha to be reunited with the Pandavas and his dear wife Draupadi. Draupadi, being piqued by the news of Arjuna's marriage, enquired from him, "What transpired? You got married to Subhadra?" She expressed her heart saying, "The bond between us will certainly loosen now, with someone else in between, just like a rope which is bound to a stack of cloth loosens if another rope is tied." But Arjuna assured her of Subhadra's decorousness. Subhadra, by the grace of Sri Krishna, conquered Draupadi's heart by her pleasing behaviour, sweet interactions, and respectful disposition, always acknowledging her seniority as Arjuna's elder wife.

In this way, the master-mind Mukunda by His intricate strategies achieved many goals. He fulfilled Arjuna's desire of marrying Subhadra. By this, He also protected Subhadra from Duryodhana. Furthermore, He awarded Arjuna the great charity of accepting the responsibility of Subhadra. With this relationship, the Pandavas became very close allies with the Yadavas. Thus Arjuna became Mukunda's partner in the act of establishing *sudharma*.

Just imagine if Duryodhana, the personification of Kali and Subhadra, the personification of material energy, were to get together! It would have been one of the most inconceivable and bizarre combinations. Lord Balarama acted as a catalyst to dramatise the event further, by feigning to arrange the marriage of Duryodhana and Subhadra. And Madhava effortlessly altered the script by aiding Arjuna's abduction of His own sister.

At the time of His advent, Yadunatha had requested the demigods to assist Him by appearing in the Yadu clan. Wherever and whenever there is a decline in religious principles, Madhava appears along with His personal associates and many demigods. Subhadra, being the power of material nature and Arjuna, being Sri Krishna's eternal associate as Nara, got married to each other. Seeing this gave Sri Krishna supreme contentment and pleasure.

By assenting to the abduction, Padmanabha endorsed another issue about marriages without consent of the partners. Should the bride be uninterested and willing to break the norm, then with the sanction of *dharma*, Sri Krishna was willing to help by uniting her with the bridegroom of her choice.

In this case, both Subhadra and Arjuna had mutual affection for each other. And for the sake of one elder, Subhadra would have had to suffer the eventuality of marrying the impious Duryodhana while she had already given her heart to the virtuous

Arjuna. Hence Sri Krishna orchestrated all this. Eventually Arjuna and Subhadra were happy, Balarama was pacified and the imperious Yadavas, who at first, were ready to attack Arjuna, became his best friends.

chapter 7

THE FIRE BEGINS

After Arjuna's return from exile, as time elapsed, Draupadi gave birth to five admirable sons; one through each of the Pandavas. Prativindhya was born of Yudhisthira; Sutasoma from Bhima; Srutakarma from Arjuna; and Satanika and Srutasena from Nakula and Sahadeva respectively. Their education commenced under the auspices of sage Dhaumya, while Arjuna personally took the responsibility of training them in all kinds of weapons.

As the reign of the Pandavas flourished, the greatness of Yudhisthira also spread far and wide. Dwarkadhish visited the Pandavas at their kingdom in Indraprastha again. Once, when He and Arjuna, with their big entourage, were camping by the Yamuna, enjoying her beauty and pleasant breeze, a very effulgent *brahmana* arrived, requesting them for a satisfying meal. Both readily offered to feed him whatever he pleased. That *brahmana* identified himself as Agnideva, the fire god, and expressed his desire to consume the forest of Khandava, while sharing his concern over how Indra constantly obstructed his attempts to save his friend Takshaka, a great snake, who lived in that forest.

Arjuna agreed but requested Agni to give him some means to successfully carry out this mission. Thus Agni offered him *Agniratha*, the famous chariot of Arjuna, the *Gandiva* bow and two inexhaustible quivers, while Sri Krishna was offered *Sudarshana chakra*.

As the mighty Purushottama and Arjuna began assisting Agni to consume the entire forest, many inmates tried to flee, but they were dropped back into the Khandava forest fire by the powerful duo. Indra tried everything in his might to stop the fire, but the son of Pandu was unstoppable. Takshaka's wife perished in the forest fire, but she and Indra saved her son Ashwasena, whom Arjuna eventually killed during the battle of Kurukshetra. This incident ignited Takshaka's wrath towards the Pandavas and he eventually took the life of Parikshit, the grandson of Arjuna and Subhadra.

No demon could withstand the power of the two friends, Sri Krishna and Arjuna. They allowed Agnideva to burn the entire forest to his complete satisfaction. During the forest fire, Sri Krishna was about to slay one of the demons, Mayasura but he cleverly took shelter of Arjuna. Seeing this, Sri Krishna protected the demon, so as to glorify His devotee Arjuna.

On being thus sheltered, he addressed Kuntinandana Arjuna, "You have protected me from the great fire and wrath of Yadunatha, therefore ask for a benediction from me." Arjuna replied, "O King of the Asuras, I have only performed my duty, I cannot ask anything from you. I can only pray for your auspiciousness. Please leave this place. You can always maintain your affection for me and we will also maintain affection towards you."

Mayasura replied, "Whatever you said is befitting great personalities like yourself, but out of love I want to perform some service to you. I am the architect of the demons, so I understand the entire science of *Vastu*. Having built many wonderful palaces for numerous demons, I wish to build a beautiful palace for you."

Arjuna replied, "O Mayasura! You have been protected by me and therefore you want to do something for me, but I cannot accept any service from you. At the same time, I don't want you to be upset, so let your desire be fulfilled. Therefore, please do something for Govinda." Then Mayasura approached Govinda and requested Him to give him some service.

Govinda contemplated and then said, "If you want to do something for Me, then build a palace for Yudhisthira that is unmatched on the earthly plane as well as on the planets of the demigods." Mayasura was very pleased to build a most astounding piece of architecture, which was ten kilometres long and equally wide. While the construction was in progress, Yadunatha thought of returning to Dwarka. He took permission from His dear sister Subhadra and the priest of the Pandavas, Dhaumya.

As the Lord was passing through Hastinapura, Yudhisthira Maharaja, personally taking the reins of the chariot, started riding. Madhusudana's friend Arjuna sat on the chariot, fanning Him with a beautiful white *chamara*. Other brothers also took turns and began fanning and serving Him with different paraphernalia. Realizing Dwarkadhish was returning, Arjuna was feeling great distress and he embraced his most dear friend. The Lord touched the feet of Yudhisthira and Bhima. And as juniors, Nakula and Sahadeva touched the feet of the Lord.

Just as Dwarkadhish had walked two paces, Yudhisthira Maharaja again beseeched Him not to go. Thereafter, He again touched the feet of Yudhisthira and begged him to be allowed to leave for Dwarka. Yudhisthira finally consented. Due to their unlimited love for Him, the Pandavas were completely distraught with His departure for Dwarka. The desire of the Pandavas that He remain ever-present in their vision could not be fulfilled. Their minds and hearts were so attached to Him that it was as though they left for Dwarka as well. Thus, Sri Krishna reached Dwarka.

In the meanwhile, Mayasura, seeking permission from the Pandavas, went to the planet of Lord Shiva and got very beautiful jewels and a conch from there. He also got a mace which was as powerful as hundred thousand maces put together and as good as the *Gandiva* bow. He offered the *Devadatta* conch to Arjuna and the mace to Bhima. Mayasura built the most impressive palace and offered it as a gift to Yudhisthira Maharaja. Its mammoth construction took just under fourteen months and this could only be possible by the grace of Shyamsundar. This *Maya sabha*, sparked a new forest fire, the blazing fire of envy in the hearts of the Kurus.

There are many lessons to be learnt from this episode of the burning of the Khandava forest.

We see how Agni represents the *Rudra tattva*, the architect of destruction. We also learn how destruction plays a vital role in the process of creation, which is followed by maintenance and then destruction again. Destruction is not an isolated principle; it is an integral part of creating a new order. Therefore, even in the working of the universal creation, there is the concept of *samhara* or *pralaya*, the great dissolution, as destruction brings forth new creation.

It is naive to expect everything to go hunky-dory in this world. To bring things to certain order, destruction is inevitable. Just as any old structure, although of some sentimental value, is demolished before creating a new one. Every new creation requires destruction. Though painful, it is rewarding in the ultimate sense.

Therefore, Agnideva consuming the entire forest was not simply coincidental; the hand of providence was at work weaving together a larger plan, so that new creation could take place. Therefore, Arjuna and Sri Krishna, backed Agnideva with their strength, and consequently he grew more powerful.

Forest connotes - variety, abstractness, uncertainty and unfolding of many things because of its unlimited variety. Similarly, the life of the Pandavas was likened to an experience of a forest.

The burning of the forest led to the creation of the *maya* palace or the palace of illusion, which was the cause of Duryodhana's unlimited envy, and also served as an instrument for Duryodhana being ridiculed by some members of the Pandavas. He left the palace with great indignation and malice in his heart towards the Pandavas, determined to avenge the insult.

Thus, in one sense, this was the place where the seed for establishing *dharma* sprouted, the demons' wrath was ignited, and the *dharmik* people, the Pandavas, had to symbolically experience the fire in the form of unlimited tests to assist Murari in establishing *dharma*.

Later, Indra told Shyamsundar to ask him for a benediction. In reality, what benediction could Indra offer Him? But it was the Lord's kindness that He simply asked for the benediction of increased affection towards Arjuna. This is His beauty. This feeling of being loved is the greatest protection the Pandavas could feel, that the Lord Himself was asking for such a benediction.

So if the demigods offer us benedictions, there is no harm. We should only ask this, "May our affection increase for the supreme object of our love, Vrajendranandana and for His service!"

chapter 8
JARASANDHA'S DREAM AND LIFE SHATTERED

Purushottama wanted to stir the innate envy of the opposing *adharmik* forces seeing the Pandavas' rise to prosperity and make them openly challenge the Pandavas. However, Yudhisthira Maharaja was not disposed to grow heedlessly, at the cost of stepping on others.

Hence Madhava inspired Narada Muni, who came to Yudhisthira Maharaja from *Pitriloka*, the land of the forefathers. Narada Muni informed him that his father, Pandu, being stuck in *Pitriloka*, desired that a *Rajasuya* sacrifice be performed. Yudhisthira Maharaja, being deeply aggrieved on hearing about his father, asked Narada Muni the cause for this. "If you perform the *Rajasuya* sacrifice, then your father will ascend to the higher realm", declared Narada Muni. Yudhisthira Maharaja, being conscientious, decided to discuss the matter with others concerned.

Most of his relatives and ministers encouraged him to proceed with the sacrifice. But Yudhisthira Maharaja wanted Giridhari's verdict. Meanwhile, in Dwarka, Narada Muni informed Giridhari about Yudhisthira's desire.

As Dwarkadhish was preparing to visit Hastinapura, one *brahmana* approached Him, on behalf of all the kings who were imprisoned by Jarasandha, entreating Him for their deliverance. The Yadava clan was willing to attack Jarasandha and kill him. But Dwarkadhish took Uddhava's counsel, who very expertly opined that it would be more appropriate for the Pandavas headed by Bhima to strike Jarasandha, as the Yadavas were not ordained by destiny to do so. Dwarkadhish, appreciating Uddhava's advice, decided to proceed to Hastinapura.

When Dwarkadhish arrived, Yudhisthira Maharaja welcomed Him warmly. He then supplicated, "My relatives are insisting that I perform this sacrifice, but I see it as a tall ask. Many are advising me to do so, as they do not see any fault in me out of affection; while others are insisting simply out of their selfish interest, as whatever benefits me will eventually benefit them. Dear Mukunda, since You are most unattached, free from greed and anger, therefore only You can adequately guide me towards my ultimate good."

Having heard Yudhisthira's plea patiently, the Lord agreed that he should perform the *Rajasuya* sacrifice. To action this plan, He then delineated to him the present state of turmoil in Bharat Varsha, the land of India. Jarasandha was aspiring to become *samrata*, the king of the kings, and to this effect, he had abducted ninety-five kings and wanted to offer them in a sacrifice to Kala Bhairava. Unfortunately Jarasandha also had the support of many kings, including Sri Krishna's father-in-law, Bhishmaka.

Ghanashyam cleverly indicated to Yudhisthira that unless Jarasandha was killed, it was impossible to perform the *Rajasuya yagya*. Yudhisthira became very much disheartened. Seeing this, Bhima intervened with encouraging words, "Madhusudana has a strategy, I have the strength and Arjuna has the power of victory, so we can easily defeat Jarasandha." And to Madhusudana, he said, "Yudhisthira's victory is ensured if he takes shelter of Your intelligence."

Dwarkadhish further elucidated five essential qualities of a *samrata* or Emperor:

a) Conqueror of enemies

32

b) Able administrator of subjects

c) Performer of all kinds of *tapasyas* or austerities

d) Prosperous

e) Strategic

Mukunda urged, "Yudhisthira, you have all these qualities. Unless the captive kings, who have lost any desire to live, are released from the clutches of Jarasandha, by eventually destroying him, it is not possible to perform the *Rajasuya yagya*." Yudhisthira Maharaja did not wish to send his brothers along with Sri Krishna to Magadha, the place of Jarasandha. Apprehensively, he said, "My dear Keshava, verily You are my mind, and Bhima and Arjuna are my two eyes. Without my mind and eyes, how will I continue to survive?"

Arjuna responded gravely, "It is the greatest sin for the powerful to act meek and bewildered. Therefore, one who desires victory should give up such attitude. If we do not perform this *yagya*, then we will be exposed as being feeble. It is our duty to release the bound kings and kill Jarasandha, or else we would rather don the garb of a *sannyasi*, a renunciant."

Pleased to hear Arjuna, Vanamali responded, "It is very encouraging to see Arjuna display character befitting the son of Kunti. No one knows when death strikes nor have we ever heard that those who never go to battle remain immortal." Vanamali assured Yudhisthira that Jarasandha could be killed without killing even one soldier. He proposed a strategy. Jarasandha, being very devoted to the *brahmanas*, never refused them any charity. Thus disguised as *brahmanas*, if Yadunatha were to beg for a charity of personal combat, Jarasandha would readily accede.

The thought of the Lord willing to beg for their sake mortified Yudhisthira. With eyes brimming with tears, he permitted Sri

Krishna, Bhima and Arjuna to proceed for the special combat.

Disguised as *brahmanas*, eventually they arrived in Magadha, waiting to receive the charity of combat. Jarasandha was offering many variegated charities. When it was Hari's turn to beg, Jarasandha was shocked to hear the unique plea of these *brahmanas* looking like *kshatriyas*.

When Jarasandha agreed, Sri Krishna presented their real identities and asked him for the choice of his opponent. Jarasandha thought Yadunatha was less of a match, Him having fled the battle once and Arjuna being younger was not an ideal choice. Hence he chose Bhima for a combat.

The fight between Bhima and Jarasandha ensued for many days; neither Bhima nor Jarasandha decisively showing any signs of victory. Janardhana knew that Jarasandha could only be killed if split into two as he was born when the demoness Jara had joined the two lifeless halves of a human body she had discovered in a forest. Bhaktavatsala, the protector of the Pandavas, cued this secret to Bhima, by splitting a blade of grass. Bhima instantly understood and spilt Jarasandha into two, thus slaying him and his ambition along with it.

On the throne of Magadha, Hari installed the son of Jarasandha, who became an ally of the Pandavas in future conflicts. Hari then released all the imprisoned kings, who were meek and humble. This incident, orchestrated by the Lord, achieved two results - it revealed the glories and valour of the Pandavas as they vanquished one of the biggest threats in their *dharmik* conquest and it won the sympathy, gratitude and friendship of the released kings towards the Pandavas.

By advising Yudhisthira to perform the *Rajasuya* sacrifice, the supreme controller Purushottama protected the Pandavas in many ways. Firstly, He encouraged Yudhisthira, fortifying his confidence to fulfill his father's desire for the *Rajasuya* sacrifice. Secondly, it removed the obstacle of insurmountable Jarasandha, and lastly, it gave a platform for Yudhisthira to glorify Dwarkadhish in the future *Agrapuja* during the *Rajasuya* sacrifice.

As they returned to Hastinapura, all the Pandavas proceeded in different directions to inform kings of their desire to perform the *Rajasuya* sacrifice. Most of the kings accepted the proposal, and those who did not accept, had to fight the Pandavas. Eventually, all of them consented.

The *Rajasuya* sacrifice was intended to achieve objectives in three spheres – familial, political and spiritual. Yudhisthira Maharaja, as a filial obligation to fulfill his father's desire, wanted to perform this *Rajasuya* sacrifice. Politically, he wanted this sacrifice to unite all those opposed to the cause of *dharma*, which was the primary cause of the Lord's advent. And spiritually, Yudhisthira desired to reveal the supremacy and the power of the Supreme Personality of Godhead, Sri Krishna publicly. Thus conducting this *yagya* satisfied the individual objective, the collective social aspect and the highest spiritual aim of worshipping Vrajendranandana.

Out of affection, Dinabandhu became completely subservient to the Pandavas. He was more often seen in Indraprastha than in His own kingdom, Dwarka. This is how the Lord performs His human-like pastimes when He appears in this world, by becoming subservient to the will of His pure devotees, and by doing everything for their pleasure, which in turn benefits the entire world.

chapter 9
RAJASUYA SACRIFICE

Yudhisthira Maharaja was very fortunate to commence the *Rajasuya* sacrifice with Srila Vyasadeva as the chief priest for the sacrificial ceremony. Among other esteemed personalities, were the great grandsire Bhishmadeva, his teacher Dronacharya and their *kula-guru* Kripacharya. And most of all, the Supreme Lord Sri Krishna Himself was present, guiding and assisting him, ensuring everything ran smoothly.

Many stalwarts present volunteered for different services; but Dinabandhu Himself took the service of washing the feet of all the saintly guests who arrived at Hastinapura to participate in the extraordinary *Rajasuya* sacrifice. It was very heartening to see that Dinabandhu took the service of washing feet. When the Lord Himself washed the feet of His devotees, the saintly people, there was no question whatsoever of any saint causing any disturbance in the *Rajasuya* sacrifice due to the difference of opinions. Every guest who came was fascinated to see Him perform this task, and hence no one complained about anything.

One part of the *Rajasuya* sacrifice was *Agrapuja* - the first offering of worship to someone, usually the greatest personality, and to all others thereafter. The Pandavas voted that Shyamsundar be worshipped for the *Agrapuja*. Bhishmadeva also chose Shyamsundar as the object of first worship. Sri Krishna kindly accepted the proposal.

But unfortunately, Krishna's cousin Shishupala, who was envious of Him since birth, vehemently opposed the proposal. He forcefully presented many reasons why Keshava should not be worshipped. Everybody tried to convince him about Sri Krishna's

36

greatness, but Shishupala persisted. Mukunda eventually took His *Sudarshana Chakra* and cut off Shishupala's head. By doing so, Mukunda, in one sense protected Shishupala who was one of His eternal servants, Jaya and Vijaya in the Vaikuntha planet. By cutting the head of Shishupala, He expedited the process of *dharma sthapana*, establishing of *dharma*.

The slaying of Shishupala in the *Rajasuya* sacrifice greatly perturbed Yudhisthira Maharaja. On completion of the sacrifice, he humbly inquired from Vyasadeva, "Why did this inauspicious activity transpire in the assembly of the *Rajasuya*?"

Srila Vyasdeva replied, "You will be an instrument for a great war that will take place thirteen years from now and those who are against the Supreme Personality of Godhead and against *dharma*, will all perish." Perceiving that he would be responsible for the death of so many people, Yudhisthira Maharaja got distressed and therefore vowed never ever to disregard the words of his superiors.

Actually Vyasadeva had not mentioned that Yudhisthira will be responsible for the war, but rather indicated that he would only be an instrument of the supreme will. Yudhisthira desired to avoid all conflicts, hence vowed never to disregard the words of his superiors, headed by Dhritarashtra. Thus the essence of Vyasadeva's cryptically spoken words remained indecipherable to Yudhisthira's intelligence.

So the Kauravas exploited this vow by inviting the Pandavas for a gambling match. At that time, Dwarkadhish was in Dwarka fighting the great demon Salva. This was a phenomenal turn of events, as foreseen by Him. This very vow of Yudhisthira became the greatest catalyst in creating a situation of grossest *adharma* on the planet, which made the Lord descend with fury and terminate all the evil forces. This act of gambling put the

Pandavas in the most difficult of times, and how they handled it, and matured from it, is another aspect of Murari's protection, inconspicuously so.

Whenever there is marginal decline in the religious principles, the time factor itself adjusts it, however when the magnitude of the decline is colossal then the Lord Himself advents to establish *dharma*.

chapter 10
GAMBLING, & DRAUPADI– THE GREATEST JEWEL OF SRI KRISHNA

When Duryodhana returned from the *Rajasuya* sacrifice, he had become like a volcano of envy witnessing the success of the Pandavas. He depicted the events he saw in the *yagya* to his father, clearly mentioning, "Krishna and Arjuna are like soulmates. Whatever Arjuna requests, He fulfills. Madhava can even renounce His highest planet for the sake of His friend Arjuna. And undoubtedly Arjuna will lay down his life for Madhava".

Duryodhana threatened to give up his life if he could not make the wealth of the Pandavas his own. The crafty Shakuni then plotted to defeat the Pandavas by virtue of a gambling match thus seizing all their possessions. Dhritarashtra acceded to this contemptible idea and ordered Vidura to bring the Pandavas for the gambling match. Vidura warned Dhritarashtra of the ill effects of gambling; however the blind king was greedy as well as heartless, and wanted to please his equally tyrannical son by all means.

Dhritarashtra enjoined the Pandavas to visit Hastinapura for a gambling match. This put Yudhisthira Maharaja in conflict, contemplating whether to visit Hastinapura to lose all that was earned by the grace of Purushottama, or to just neglect the invitation thus disobeying his superiors and breaking his vow of following whatever the superiors ask of him.

He seeked Vidura's counsel, who told him, "You have to follow your heart." Although here Yudhisthira apparently acted like an ordinary person, his vow itself was that of an extraordinary person. Viewing the situation as ordained by destiny, he proceeded to Hastinapura.

As the gambling match began, Yudhisthira started losing everything, beginning with his wealth to his own brothers. At last, when Shakuni asked him to stake his wife Draupadi, as if robbed of his own intelligence, Yudhisthira agreed. This was unprecedented. Even the great king Nala who lost everything in the gambling arena, had walked away in rage when asked by his brother to stake his wife Damayanti.

When Yudhisthira staked Draupadi, no one objected. Everyone, including Bhishma, Drona, Kripa, and the other Pandavas, became inert, like dead stones. And the vicious Dhritarashtra relished all the while.

This entire incident, with its oppressive series of events and overwhelming emotions was one of the most challenging episodes of the *Mahabharata*. Herein Vidura, *Dharmaraja* and almost everyone was following *dharma*, which meant following the orders of the superiors.

Yudhisthira Maharaja was following the *dharma* of respect and of a *kshatriya*, who cannot disregard a challenge. The other Pandavas were following their *dharma* of respect towards their eldest brother. Bhishmadeva executed the *dharma* of a loyal citizen of Hastinapura, so even though he knew what was right and wrong, he could not stop the gambling match. Karna was loyal to his friend and was revengeful as well. Dronacharya was loyal, being an employee of Duryodhana. Dhritarashtra was completely bound out of fatherly affection towards his son.

In this way, everyone assembled during the gambling match had some *dharma* or the other, but all these *dharmas* were in conflict with each other. The *dharma* of brotherhood of the Pandavas was conflicting with their *pati-dharma* of protecting their wife. Verily, their adherence to '*dharma*' became the cause of greatest *adharma* in the history of Mahabharata.

When the Pandavas had lost everything, Duryodhana demanded that Draupadi be dragged down to the arena. Karna provoked him further, insinuating that it did not matter whether she was clothed or naked before them, because after all, she was a 'prostitute' sharing five husbands. Thus Draupadi was brought down to the assembly of the unscrupulous.

Dushasana began mercilessly disrobing Draupadi. Like a destitute, she expectantly gaped at the entire assembly of the most powerful individuals, but none came to her rescue. Unfortunately, all were fallible. Some wanted her to be naked; others were helplessly sympathetic. Even though some, like Dronacharya, were powerful enough to punish the wicked simply by cursing, no one could save her dignity. In spite of having so many well-wishers in the assembly, none could actually protect Draupadi in the hour of dire need.

This story elucidates how, despite the availability of resources, one is incapable of protecting oneself at all times, as those very resources may render themselves useless if ordained by destiny.

Draupadi, having maintained her *patni-dharma* of being respectful to her husbands, and her *kula-dharma* of being respectful as a daughter-in-law of Kuru-clan, submissively asked Bhishmadeva, "Was Yudhisthira Maharaja right in gambling me away?" Nobody could answer her question nor offer her protection. She was neither looking for answers, nor begging for her life to be protected. Her plea was to protect her priceless dignity, her devotion towards Yadunatha and her determination to endure for the future.

It was the most crucial and difficult predicament, but even in such a state, Draupadi implored Sri Krishna, with a grateful heart, not just in distress - "O Krishna! O Dwarkanatha! Please come and protect me. O Dwarkavasi Sri Krishna! O Gopala! O Gopijana Vallabha! O Keshava! These Kauravas are insulting me, while You are unaware. O Natha! O Ramanatha! O Brajanatha! O Janardhana! I am drowning in the ocean of Kauravas, please protect me. You are Sachidananda Rupa! Mahayogin! Vishwatma! Vishwabhavan! Govinda! Please release me from this difficulty."

The Supreme Lord Krishna could hear the cry of Draupadi, even while He was on the battlefield fighting the demon Salva. The Supreme Knower of all, decided to extend His protection to her. As Draupadi was fervently beseeching Govinda, Dushasana was vehemently trying to disrobe her. However, he was unsuccessful due to Sri Krishna's merciful reciprocation in the form of unlimited cloth, which was protecting Draupadi.

If the Lord benedicts someone to be blessed unlimitedly, then how much can anyone take away from him? In her plight, Draupadi, while retaining her loyalty to her husbands, called out to Sri Krishna and He indeed came and protected Draupadi's dignity, chastity and shyness. Devakinandana provided more and more cloth for Draupadi, as Dushasana tried to disrobe her more and more, ultimately leading Dushasana to complete exhaustion. In the tug-of-war between Sri Krishna's protection and Dushasana's efforts, Dushasana fell unconscious.

The Kurus wanted to destroy the confidence of the Pandavas forever, and create strife among them, but they failed. And the Pandavas were steeped in regret and remorse, though they felt cheated, but at no point of time were they upset or angry with Sri Krishna. They stood the test of time and strengthened their confidence and exhibited how one can overcome any obstacle, by the grace of the Lord.

This was the victory of Draupadi's confidence in Madhava's protection. Her *dharma* was victorious, her loyalty was victorious, her chastity was victorious, and her seeking shelter of Madhava was victorious. What adverse hardship she had to endure to demonstrate this principle! Through this story, Madhava teaches that at the level of the heart, as well as the soul, it is only He who can really protect. It was only He who protected Draupadi. Not only did He protect Draupadi's dignity, He also protected the confidence of the Pandavas.

chapter II

SRI KRISHNA MEETS THE PANDAVAS IN THE FOREST

After facing the tribulation of losing everything in the gambling arena, Draupadi and the Pandavas were sent to the forest. Vanamali was extremely agonized on hearing this account. He came to meet them and indignantly expressed, "O Yudhisthira, I think Mother Bhumi will drink the blood of Duryodhana, Dushasana, Shakuni and Karna. We will reinstate you on the throne of Hastinapura, by punishing those involved in this foul play. Wiping out such anti-social crooks is actual upholding of religious principles!"

As the Pandavas heard the affectionate outburst, they became overwhelmed. Arjuna offered his heartfelt prayers to Sri Krishna, glorifying Him as the Supreme Brahman.

In some time, the despondent Draupadi came forth, streams of tears gushing incessantly, her heart aching as she woefully questioned Sri Krishna – "How is that I, the sister of Dhrishtadyumna and wife of the Pandavas, had to face such a trying situation? I am the wife of such great heroes, but none of them could protect me. To hell with the great *Gandiva* bow of Arjuna! To hell with the great mace of Bhima which could not protect! Krishna! Even You weren't there to protect me? I am Your friend, Your kin. Wasn't it Your responsibility to protect us? I am the fire-born daughter of Drupada and You were capable of protecting me."

Interestingly, Ghanashyam abstained from reminding Draupadi of His protection through unlimited cloth. Instead, He said, "The wives of the men who are responsible for your anguish shall soon shed tears at the death of their husbands. O Draupadi! The sky may fall apart, the mountains may come crashing down, Mother Earth may rupture, but I vow that these words of Mine shall come to pass." Arjuna consoled Draupadi, "Do not lament. Be assured that Sri Krishna's words are like lines etched on stone."

Hari expressed that had He been present in that assembly, He would have surely stopped the gambling match by requesting the senior Kurus. And if they had not relented, He would have demolished their clan. However, by the will of providence, He was busy fighting Salva and could not undo the happenings. The Supreme Absolute, Adideva, behaved as though confined by providence and hence personally could not extend His protection due to being held up on the battlefield. This human-like behaviour on behalf of the Supreme enhances the affectionate dealings of His devotees towards Him.

This interaction is unparalleled, as it was extremely poignant, and steeped with loving affection and gratitude. Vanamali heartily sympathised with the Pandavas, not as the Supreme Absolute but as their ever well-wisher. He expressed displeasure at Draupadi's anguish at the hands of the Kurus and exceedingly so because even the Pandavas were in a quandary at that time. Mukunda felt deeply remorseful for the apparent failure to protect Draupadi Himself while completely guarding the secret of His protection in the form of that unending cloth as she was being disrobed.

Draupadi felt somewhat pacified. Despite the reversals, she never abandoned her friendship with Yadunatha. Even though empty handed, she offered her tears full of gratitude and affection to Shyamsundar as He was returning to Dwarka. And Prananatha, the Lord of His devotees' hearts, gladly accepted her offering like a *chakora* bird, who patiently tolerates the severe pangs of thirst only to quench it from pure rain water.

Prananatha felt responsible for Draupadi's woe. This greatly reassured Draupadi, who worshiped Him with tears of love. Neither did the Lord object to the outburst of the loving protection demanded by Draupadi nor did He remind her of the protection He had de facto provided. Instead, He reassured her of the Kurus' ultimate destination due to their deplorable actions.

This is another kind of protection - the protection she received on being affectionately angry towards her object of love, Dwarkadhish. Love means responsibility, which He wholeheartedly accepted for Draupadi's situation, thus conveying His immense love for the Pandavas.

Sincere devotees never expect their Lord to churn out miracles, one after another like a magician. They teach us how to live in this world amidst dualities and setbacks while never compromising their affection for the Lord.

This incident was actually meant to cause a rift between Draupadi and the Pandavas. But instead, Draupadi, whose devotion unto Sri Krishna grew manifold through these reverses, incidentally acted as an instrument in getting the Pandavas to bond more intimately. She became the very purpose and cause of their existence.

chapter 12
PROSPERITY IN THE FOREST

Dinabandhu extended his unconditional protection to the Pandavas in many ways. He once did so by strategically informing Dhritarashtra about His visit to the Pandavas and His vow to destroy the Kurus, thereby instilling constant fear in his heart and shattering his confidence. This message was narrated by Sanjaya to Dhritarashtra - "Sri Krishna has offered to be Arjuna's charioteer during the imminent battle. Parthasarathi has also pledged to kill all those responsible for this *adharma*, headed by Duryodhana, Shakuni and Karna." Hearing this, Dhritarashtra lamented, "Vidura had warned me that all my sons would perish, having participated in this immoral act of gambling. I knew this would eventuate one day." Thus the perennial fear of losing his sons became Dhritarashtra's reality.

CONFIDENCE THROUGH MANY SAGES

Once the sage Dhaumya painted a cryptic picture, divulging some details about the future war and its consequences to Yudhisthira, saying, "The war, which is like a blazing fire will be extinguished by the cloud personified as Arjuna, and stimulated by the wind personified as Sri Krishna, making it rise up in the sky. Divine weapons used in the war will be the lightning, white horses will be like ducks in a row, *Gandiva* will resemble the rainbow, Indra's bow; and the angry *Gandiva* will shower arrows on the blazing fire of Karna, making the fire of war extinguish."

MEETING AT PRABHASA

Sri Krishna and Balarama met the Pandavas again in Prabhasa, the holy place where they were performing austerities. At that

47

ume, Keshava stirred the spirit of *dharma* in Yudhisthira by provoking him with a suggestion of completing the exile without actually going through it for the stipulated time frame of twelve years and one year incognito. But the virtuous Yudhisthira, spontaneously rejected the proposal, determined to honour his word and complete the stipulated exile term, without Sri Krishna's help. Hari was pleased with Yudhisthira's nobility and scrupulousness. An unalloyed devotee is certainly eager for the Lord's protection but not at the cost of breaking the principles of *dharma*. The devotee, being fixed in his vows, also strives to protect the Lord from being perceived as being unreasonably partial to His devotees.

Meanwhile, Sri Balarama, lamenting the plight of the Pandavas expressed, "Though the Pandavas are *dharmik* they are suffering while the immoral people are enjoying dictatorship." To this, Satyaki responded, "It is not the time to mourn; we have to act against the Kurus." Satyaki, a worthy disciple of his dear guru, Arjuna, was willing to fight for the truth. Sri Krishna then said, "O magnanimous Satyaki! These words are befitting you, but Yudhisthira shall not give up his *dharma* bypassing his word of honour, for the sake of anything that is not self earned."

Hearing Madhusudana, Yudhisthira said, "Satyaki, what you mentioned is natural to you, but for me protection of the truth is more important than acquiring a kingdom. Hari knows this very well. He knows me and I also know His constitutional position. It was our great fortune to have your association, now you all may go to Dwarka, and soon we shall meet during the war."

DRAUPADI'S CONFIDENCE

Later during the exile, Jayadratha the infamous son-in-law of Dhritarashtra, who was as abusive as his brothers-in-law, Dushasana and Duryodhana, attempted to abduct Draupadi.

When Jayadratha tried seducing her, approaching her as if she were promiscuous, Draupadi rebuked him, warning that it would cost him his dear life if he didn't leave immediately.

Nevertheless, when Jayadratha forcibly dragged her onto his chariot, the helpless Draupadi called out to the Pandavas, being assured of their protection. Draupadi thought, "I dare beg for mercy from Jayadratha, since I have full faith in My Lord Sri Krishna. Driving Arjuna's chariot, He will soon come looking for me. Certainly the two of them together are invincible; even Indra cannot dream of winning against them."

She condemned Jayadratha, "Positively, Yadunatha along with Arjuna and the other Yadavas will rescue me. And be assured that Arjuna will not spare you from his arrows. You will then deplore your own futile intelligence!"

This reaction from Draupadi is awe-inspiring. Despite being so precariously placed - brutally abducted and facing a possible molestation, she maintained her staunch conviction and faith in the protection of Madhava and Arjuna. This reveals that Brajanatha fortified her faith, even more so in times of adversity. In her helplessness, she experienced greater shelter and confidence. She maintained her dignity, confidence and devotion, not even considering the thought of begging for mercy from a low-class person like Jayadratha.

Certainly, this paid off. Arjuna and Bhima came and trashed the low-minded Jayadratha. They wanted to give him death penalty but Yudhisthira requested them not to kill him since he was the husband of their only sister Dushala, the daughter of Dhritarashtra. Of course, this did not change the incorrigible Jayadratha, rather he became revengeful and eventually, a cause of great distress for the Pandavas.

DURVASA MUNI RUNS AWAY

Wandering about in the forest, the Pandavas were learning from many sages. Once, Duryodhana diabolically decided to send Durvasa Muni to the place of the Pandavas in the forest. Thus far, all his efforts to destroy the Pandavas had failed miserably. Episodes like the poisoning attempt, the plot of burning them alive, a shot at disrobing their very dignity and the constant pursuit of denting their confidence were all in vain. On the other hand, the Pandavas kept growing confident and collecting blessings, while simultaneously developing an affectionate bond with the Supreme Personality of Godhead, Sri Krishna. Hence, the envious Duryodhana thought that the best way to destroy the Pandavas was to make them the object of a great sage's curse.

Duryodhana was quite adept at pleasing saintly personalities. He did please Durvasa Muni, but did not ask any benediction for his own purity. Rather he requested Durvasa Muni to go to the Pandavas after Draupadi, who usually ate last, had already honoured her meal.

As it was well known, the Sun God had gifted the "*Akshaya Patra*", the inexhaustible pot to the Pandavas to feed hundreds and thousands of young students who followed Yudhisthira Maharaja when they were in the forest. But it had one clause; the pot would stop producing for that day after Draupadi had taken her meal. Thus, Durvasa Muni, along with his ten thousand disciples, came to the forest and requested the Pandavas to feed them. He then went to bathe in the River Yamuna.

Draupadi became apprehensive, wondering how she could feed ten thousand disciples of Durvasa Muni after she had already taken her meal. It seemed impossible. She also realized that failing to do so would mean committing an offense unto a great sage. Everything seemed futile. But she had one trump card – Her strong faith in Sri Krishna, and so she promptly began remembering Him, the slayer of Kamsa, calling out, "O Krishna! O Mahaprabhu! O Devakinandana! O Vasudeva! Please free us from this miserable situation of not being able to serve a great sage. Please give us your blessings. I seek Your shelter."

Draupadi remembered how Yadunatha had protected her in the assembly of the Kurus when Dushasana was trying to disrobe her. As Draupadi was remembering Dwarkadhish, He was with Rukmini. He immediately left Rukmini, and at the pace of mind reached where the Pandavas were residing. He approached Draupadi informing her that He was very hungry and needed to be fed. When Draupadi heard this, she became very embarrassed, as she was unable to fulfill His desire. It's one thing not to be in the position to feed all those sages, but here she wasn't even able to feed her Lord.

Draupadi exclaimed, "There is no food left!" Mukunda replied "Show Me the pot." On presenting Him the pot, Mukunda discovered one grain of rice, which He promptly honored, experiencing great satisfaction.

Dinanatha then told Sahadeva to invite all the sages. As Sahadeva started to walk towards them, Durvasa Muni started speaking, "I have performed a great misdeed by asking Yudhisthira Maharaja to execute this difficult task of cooking for so many. If the Pandavas get enraged because of this, we will be shattered. I still remember how, on committing an offence unto Ambarish Maharaja, I had to bear heavy consequences. Therefore, O my dear associates, I always fear the great, unalloyed devotees of Lord Hari. The Pandavas are very qualified and astute, full of *dharma*, valour and heroism, always maintaining their austerities and vows. Naturally, if they are displeased with me, then I am doomed. Therefore, let us escape this place right away."

Panicking thus, Durvasa Muni and his followers fled.

Upon reaching there, Sahadeva saw that there were no sages by the river. Upon inquiring from the local sages, they informed him how Durvasa Muni and his group had fled the place. He came back to Yudhisthira Maharaja and Sri Krishna and related everything. But the Pandavas were apprehensive with the thought that Durvasa Muni could still return any time, even at midnight. So how could they possibly be relieved of this great threat?

Then Hari told Yudhisthira Maharaja, "O Kunti Kumaras, the great Durvasa Muni is always angry, but Draupadi remembered Me and therefore I came here. Do not fear Durvasa Muni, he ran away simply by remembering your supremacy. Those who always follow the path of *dharma* should be fearless, and you are certainly following *dharma*. Now I shall return to Dwarka." As Devakinandana was about to leave, all the Pandavas told Him, "O Govinda! You always protect us. We are fortunate to experience Your shelter every time. There is no hope other than You! We bless You, may You eternally protect Your devotees and help them fulfill their desires." Thus the Pandavas blessed Dinabandhu to be the greatest well-wisher of His devotees.

Madanmohan's protection here was the benediction of being freed from a possible curse of Durvasa Muni. This was a great strategy planned by Duryodhana but Mukunda came at the opportune moment. He reminded Durvasa Muni about the folly of testing His unalloyed devotees, an incident which He had orchestrated earlier in connection to Ambarish Maharaja. As *Paramatma*, Yadunatha instigated Durvasa Muni's intelligence, reminding him of his offence to Ambarish Maharaja and his consequent predicament, and the extent to which he might suffer by offending many devotees instead of just one! Therefore the terrified Durvasa Muni fled.

He not only protected the Pandavas, but also made a special place in their heart as the *Paramatma*, always evoking them to perform the right action at the right time from within their heart. This was a very special protection extended by Ghanashyam to the Pandavas. This is another wonderful incident where Draupadi called out to Madhava in the most trying times and again protected the entire Pandava family, this time from the wrath of Durvasa Muni.

KARNA TRICKED

Karna faced the constant predicament of unsuccessful attempts at killing Arjuna. In every battle, he was defeated by Arjuna, but at the same time was protected due to his impenetrable armour.

Indra, being inspired to rob Karna's intelligence, came in the guise of a *brahmana*, begging for his armour in charity. Although being forewarned by Suryadeva, not to give his armour to any *brahmana* in charity, Karna still gave it to Indra as the armour was meant merely for Karna's self-defense and could not take Arjuna's life. In return, Karna asked for a *Shakti* weapon from him, with an intention to kill Arjuna. Indra gave the *Shakti* weapon, but also warned Karna, that the personality, whom he was meaning to kill, was ably protected by Sri Krishna and thus he would not be able to inflict any harm upon him.

Having lost his formidable armor, Karna lost his biggest asset and was now an ordinary opponent that Arjuna could not only defeat, but would eventually kill in the decisive battle of *Mahabharata*.

As the years passed, the Pandavas were concluding the period of their exile incognito for a year in the house of King of Virata, where they faced many ordeals. Arjuna had to disguise as a eunuch; Yudhisthira took the role of an advisor to King Virata; Bhima became the cook, and Nakula and Sahadeva became keepers of animals. Draupadi, the queen of the entire planet Earth, became a mere maid-servant of an insignificant queen.

While in this role, she was being harassed by that queen's brother, Kichaka. Bhima, the only one who came to know that Kichaka wanted to enjoy heavenly pleasure with Draupadi, became furious and opened the gates of hell for Kichaka, beating him to death, with his accumulated vengeance against all other offenders of Draupadi.

With each resentful blow to Kichaka, Bhima remembered the likes of Duryodhana and Jayadratha, who he had to forgive at least for the time being, on request of the virtuous and compassionate *Dharmaraja* Yudhisthira. Thus, seizing the golden opportunity of no elders intervening this time, Bhima thrashed Kichaka beyond recognition; thus releasing all his pent up anger and frustration of thirteen years for the want of justice, and also the bitterness of not having been in the position to exercise the power to punish.

Duryodhana and his party had been trying to discover the Pandavas' whereabouts. The gruesome death of Kichaka raised an alarm in the minds of many. They knew that only very few were capable of killing Kichaka and the description of his death had Bhima's signature all over it. Bhishmadeva also indirectly hinted Duryodhana about the place where the Pandavas might be living, saying, "You should look for a place where everything is going on nicely, with abundance of fruits, vegetables, grains, jewels and friendship."

Duryodhana realized that this description matched exactly with King Virata's kingdom, where Kichaka had been killed. Thus, convinced that the Pandavas were living there, they resolved to attack Virata's kingdom from both sides, along with their allies the Trigaratha brothers, aware that the Pandavas would surely join the battle to protect their hosts. Bhima fought the Trigaratha brothers while Arjuna, in the garb of a eunuch, was forced to fight on the other side, where the Kurus headed by Bhishma, Drona and Karna had attacked.

Arjuna single-handedly trounced them, rendering them all unconscious. But he spared their lives for the final combat. Duryodhana then tried convincing Bhishma that since the Pandavas had exposed themselves before completion of the stipulated time of remaining incognito; they needed to go in exile again, as per the rule. Bhishma turned down his logic, asserting that the Pandavas had spent more time in exile than required and hence their return to Indraprastha was inevitable. Duryodhana was not agreeable to this.

From this point on, the Pandavas had to take certain difficult decisions to aid the establishment of *dharma* by the Lord. These involved inconceivable actions such as raising weapons against their own teachers, uncles and even the most revered and affectionate grandfather Bhishmadeva.

One day as the Pandavas were preparing their next course of action, Sanjaya, the messenger of Dhritarashtra, arrived with a message at the quarters of Yudhisthira Maharaja that he should withdraw from this ghastly warfare, since Dhritarashtra's own sons, headed by Duryodhana were stubborn and unwilling to step down. Instead, Yudhisthira Maharaja should subsist by begging in Dwarka, since he was anyway habituated for all these years, being in exile. Also, he should avoid begging in Hastinapura for his own good; otherwise the citizens would criticize his uncle, Dhritarashtra.

This makes it evident that Dhritarashtra was so wicked that he actually seriously considered this proposal and sent Sanjaya as a messenger to inform the Pandavas about the same. Yudhisthira Maharaja responded to Sanjaya, "Let the seers tell us what is right, I cannot give up my *svadharma*. I will only act as Vasudeva Krishna advises, because He is neutral and does not take sides."

When Yudhisthira Maharaja presented this proposal to Dwarkadhish, He responded unrelentingly, comparing the Kauravas to robbers. "If a dacoit loots, he is a sinner, whether he does it with a virtuous intention or not. Duryodhana has become a dacoit and punishing him will earn you great pious credit."

Madhava said, "O Sanjaya! Draupadi implored Me for help while being disrobed in the gambling arena, but I could not come to her rescue and hence I have been in debt. And now the time to repay that debt has come." His strong words were intended to make matters crystal clear for the viewing of the blind and iniquitous Dhritarashtra.

On returning, Sanjaya conveyed this to him and also his observation of the intimate bond between Keshava and the Pandavas. He related the scene in Arjuna's residential quarters: "I saw Mukunda's two lotus feet on Arjuna's lap, and Arjuna's one foot on Draupadi's lap and other on the lap of Satyabhama, who was massaging Arjuna's foot. This is the level of intimacy in their relationship."

Here we see that the Kurus were trying to emotionally blackmail the Pandavas. Consequently, this uncharacteristic desire to flee and subsist by begging, unbefitting a true warrior, creeped into Arjuna while on the battlefield. But Purushottama extended His special protection by promptly freeing the Pandavas of such futile, *adharmik* emotions.

ARMY OR WEAPON-LESS KRISHNA

By the time Yadunatha returned to Dwarka, Duryodhana became aware of the events that transpired at Virata's place. He decided to visit Dwarka quickly to seek Dwarkadhish's assistance in the upcoming war. Arjuna also went to there hoping to be the recipient of His mercy.

Duryodhana entered Devakinandana's bedroom first and chose to directly sit by the Lord's head, while Arjuna sat by His feet. Both were waiting for the Lord to wake up. As soon as He awoke, even though the Lord saw Arjuna first, He asked Duryodhana the reason for his visit. Duryodhana said, "O Yadunatha! We are on the verge of fighting with the Pandavas and I need Your help. You are a friend to Arjuna and our friend as well. You are our relative and therefore I have come here asking for Your alliance. Please help us." Madhava told Duryodhana, "I understand you arrived first, but I saw Arjuna first. Also, since he is younger, he should be given precedence to choose."

Hari then presented Arjuna with two options. On one hand, He had hundred million *gopas* (cowherd boys), who, being His powerful expansions, were as good as Lord Narayana. Therefore they were known as the invincible '*Narayani Sena*'. On the other hand, there was Hari Himself, all alone. Also, He would neither fight in the battle nor raise a weapon including His *Sudarshana chakra*.

Keshava prompted Arjuna, "Choose whichever option you want and I will accept." Arjuna, the invincible, responded, "O Keshava! Even though You will not be fighting in the battle, You are the Supreme Lord, who has appeared amidst the *kshatriyas*. Therefore, I want You by my side." When Duryodhana heard this, he was overjoyed. He thought he had tricked Krishna, taking the entire army of the *Yadu-kula*.

After Duryodhana left, Mukunda enquired from Arjuna "Why did you choose Me even though I am not fighting? It was not a prudent decision; it seems you did not contemplate enough before deciding!" Arjuna replied, "O Govinda! You alone are sufficient to destroy the entire planet. Your grace alone qualifies and enables me to fight my enemies. My dear Lord, You are always successful. Wherever You go, success automatically follows, and since I desire victory, I chose You. It is my great desire that You be my charioteer. I want to hand over the reins of the chariot of my life to You. Please fulfill this long-standing desire of mine."

Govinda, satisfied with Arjuna's response, said, "O Partha! You always want victory and that is very good. I will certainly accept the role of your charioteer and let all your desires be fulfilled."

Thus, Shyamsundar strategically protected Arjuna by inspiring him to maintain his confidence in Him. The choice was rather tricky - hundred million soldiers on one side and a lone individual who would not even lift a single weapon on the other.

Why did Sri Krishna ask Arjuna to choose first? He did so only to increase Arjuna's glory. Although Duryodhana would have chosen the army anyway and hence the outcome would have been the same, but it could have been viewed in history as though Arjuna went ahead with the option that was naturally left for him and not out of his personal choice.

Having been given precedence to choose first, Arjuna could have been tempted by the hundred million soldiers, but without hesitation, he spontaneously chose Devakinandana, even though He was not fighting. Arjuna knew that He is the ultimate visionary, and knower of past, present and future. Action that is not backed by proper vision is futile. Besides Adideva, who could harmonize the time factor, know the perfect plan of action in various challenging situations, and suggest what the best *astra* to use is? Who would give him *sudarshana*, the best *darshan*? Considering all these factors, Arjuna accepted Parthasarathi as his guide, in the form of a charioteer.

Since Parthasarathi declined to actively participate in the battle, Balarama, understanding His heart, eventually decided not to take sides and hence neither supported Duryodhana nor Arjuna.

chapter 14

KRISHNA:
THE PEACE MAKER

All the allies of the Pandavas had gathered to discuss the future course of action. In their assembly, Yudhisthira appealed, "Let us go and request our beloved Yadunatha to visit Hastinapura for a peace talk, so that the war may altogether be avoided. By your unconditional support, we have become bold, and are unnecessarily challenging the Kurus."

So they approached Hari and requested Him to visit Hastinapura as a peacemaker. On being approached, Hari said, "I am always at your disposal. Please tell Me, how may I serve you all? I will certainly fulfill your orders." Such was His loving disposition towards the Pandavas. He would willingly do anything for them, not because He was socially obligated to them, but out of being completely subjugated by their affection.

Yudhisthira was pleased with Mukunda's response but began reflecting upon the pitfalls of the war, comparing it to a petty fight between two dogs over a dry piece of bone, as the eventuality of a possible war was discussed many times earlier during the exile.

Mukunda agreed to go to Hastinapura for a peace talk. However He encouraged Yudhisthira for the war should the peace talk fail!

KRISHNA PROVOKES BHIMA

Bhima requested Purushottama to appeal gently so as to avoid agitating the Kauravas, and concluded that He should seek for peace asking for just five villages. Having heard Bhima speak like this, Yadunatha was startled and said, "How come you are talking about peace? You were always ready to fight. Peace talks do not suit you, O mighty Bhima! This sounds like the shivering of a mountain!" He thus provoked Bhima for the right cause. Bhima then assured Yadunatha that he desired peace, but that didn't mean he was afraid of fighting.

DRAUPADI PROMISED

When Draupadi was informed that Dwarkadhish was visiting Hastinapura with a peace message, she became indignant. Reminding Him of her past woe, she declared that if the Pandavas were unwilling to fight, she would urge her elderly father, along with her sons to fight against the Kurus. Hearing her out, Bhaktavatsala responded, "O chaste Draupadi, hear My promise. Mount Himalaya may move from its place, Mother Earth may get fragmented, but be assured that all your enemies will surely perish and your husbands will eventually be coroneted"

The Pandavas were torn between fighting for justice and settling out of compassion, and were willing to forgo justice for compassion. Madhava's intention was to protect the Pandavas' vow for justice. Though Madhava was willing to accommodate an amicable settlement, He was very clear that the Kurus had to be shown the door of justice, and the Pandavas had to gain sovereignty.

When Damodara arrived at Hastinapura, Duryodhana extended Him an invitation to dine with them but He declined. Thus He insinuated His loyalty to the Pandavas.

He publicly showed affection for the Pandavas by glorifying them in presence of everyone, including Duryodhana. Damodara said, "I do not eat in the house where there is no love. Duryodhana, since you have no affection for Me, I did not accept your offering. Those who hate the Pandavas, hate Me as well and those who favour the Pandavas, favour Me. You should know for sure that the Pandavas and I are one in essence. I am willing to cut My own flesh for Arjuna, and Arjuna would do the same for Me." But Duryodhana was unmoved as he had lost all his discrimination.

Hari then met Vidura, who pleaded Him not to mediate with the Kurus, but Hari assured him that He was merely performing His duty, regardless of the outcome.

In the assembly to discuss the peace settlement, Keshava tried by all means to convince the Kurus, negotiating that the war be called off by awarding just five villages to the Pandavas. But the haughty and scornful Duryodhana, unrelentingly roared, "I shall not spare space even as much as the tip of a needle for them, what to speak of five villages!"

Actually this was Yadunatha's trick. He had knowingly placed this bait of settling for just five villages. Any fool would have consented, but Duryodhana was more than a fool. He was hell bent out of his arrogance and corrupt intelligence. He saw through Murari's scheme. He knew that if he did give them five villages, in the course of time, they would expand their territory. Thus, there could be an eventuality of him coming under their subjugation, which was an intolerable thought for Duryodhana. He preferred dying than seeing the Pandavas flourish. Hence he denied parting with even a miniscule amount of land.

Padmanabha requested the elderly Kurus to bind Duryodhana, Dushasana, Shakuni and Karna, so that the entire Kuru dynasty could be saved from the inauspicious outcome of their reckless obstinacy. But they expressed their limitation and denied doing so. On the contrary, Duryodhana ordered his soldiers to bind Adideva. Satyaki promptly divulged their plan to Sri Krishna, who pacified him. As they came to bind Him, the Lord expanded, revealing His partial universal form. Of course, Duryodhana was neither the least bit transformed nor impacted. Dhritarashtra, by

Murari's grace, could see His form, after which, he did not want to see anything else. Thus they could not bind Him.

Before departing, Dwarkadhish rode off to a secluded place with Karna on His chariot. He tried convincing Karna to stop the war by reminding him about his fraternal connection with the Pandavas. Karna was a key influential member on the Kurus' side; if he got convinced, the war would not take place. But Karna rejected the proposal and in fact requested Hari not to reveal his identity to the Pandavas. Thus, Shyamsundar realized that Karna gave more precedence to his friendship, forgetting the larger picture, which would have been beneficial to all. Thus Karna's unintelligent decision opened the doors to his imminent ill-fate.

In this way Govinda tried His best, but the peace mission failed. In line with His assurance to Draupadi, the Kurus had now sealed their fate.

Next, Dwarkadhish visited Kunti, updating her of the surety of the war. Seeing her mortified on hearing this, He consoled her. Thus reinforced, she sent strong words of encouraging advice to Yudhisthira through Sri Krishna, enjoining the Pandavas to fight the war with valour, befitting a true *kshatriya*, thus fulfilling their obligation towards their *svadharma*.

Yadunatha then returned, externally unsuccessful but internally satisfied that He did everything he could for the sake of the Pandavas, who were His life and soul.

Madhava protected the Pandavas by not revealing Karna's identity. Otherwise the Pandavas would have been in an inconceivable dilemma, fighting their eldest brother. Also Karna had persistently asserted to Him that he would only fight for Duryodhana and even if Yudhisthira were to offer him the kingdom, he would simply give it to Duryodhana. So Madhava

63

allowed destiny to take its own course, rather than personally revealing this fact and putting them in a mutually conflicting situation.

Devakinandana's untiring efforts in giving the anti-parties another chance, demonstrate how the Lord is always eager for everyone's progress, always endeavouring to direct the living entities away from their detrimental, impious resolve. He willingly bargains, asking them for a meagre price, giving heavy concessions, sending sages and teachers to convince and aid them, but unless the living entity himself acts on the path, he or she cannot progress towards positivity.

Thus the peacemaker failed, ensuring that the Pandavas would be the future kings of the entire world, establishing the kingdom of *dharma*.

chapter 15

KURUKSHETRA AND THE GITA

With the war now a surety, the Pandavas geared up for the fight. But, on the battlefield, when Yudhisthira saw the army of the Kurus, he became despondent. Seeing this, Arjuna assured his brother saying, "Our victory is guaranteed. Narada Muni has declared to us, that wherever there is Achyuta, certainly victory follows. He is infallible, and so be rest assured and give up your fear as that very Achyuta is wishing for your victory." This incident shows that even discussions about Govinda protected the Pandavas, reinforcing their waning confidence.

The Pandavas proceeded towards the battlefield, brimming with confidence in their Lord and master, Achyuta, who was leading them from the front. The Pandavas' victory was certain, but it was not without its testing moments. There is no such thing as a hassle-free victory in this world, just as there is no gain without pain. Victory without sacrifice is superficial and sacrifices for the cause of *dharma* and Sri Krishna is victory guaranteed. This was the consciousness of the Pandavas, as they stepped onto the battlefield of Kurukshetra.

BHAGAVAD-GITA

This is the heart of *Mahabharata*. Arjuna entered the battlefield with great determination; in fact just moments before he had spoken to Yudhisthira about the necessity of the war. So much so that he was instrumental in encouraging his despondent brother and in removing his doubts. But on seeing whom all he had to contend with in this decisive battle, at the stake of their own lives, Arjuna himself became completely disheartened. Observing Arjuna's distress, the benevolent Lord, out of great compassion, poured out from His heart, in the form of the most wonderful discourse, the song of God, unparalleled and replete with enlightenment.

Mathuranatha protected Arjuna from many challenging situations through the medium of *Gita*. He enabled his understanding of his duty, and his object of devotion. Arjuna thus, keeping aside his doubts, submitted and fully took shelter of Him. Arjuna was ready to act for the benefit of humanity. Jagamohana made Arjuna the instrument in establishing *dharma*, for which He had descended to this mortal world.

In essence, Hari divulged a few of life's essential truths to Arjuna. Life is so designed that we are forced to perform our duty, whether we like it or not. Like the changing seasons, which appear and disappear, we simply have to tolerate life's reversals.

One has to firstly understand, *svadharma* - occupation based on the qualities one has acquired, and then perform one's prescribed duty accordingly, without concern about victory or defeat, life or death. *Svadharma* has to be performed without attachment, because although we have the right to perform our prescribed duty, we are not entitled to the fruits of our actions and whatever *svadharma* we perform, should benefit the society. Otherwise what is the use, even if one was to accept the renounced order?

Every aspect of life is like a *yagya* or a sacrifice, and the pinnacle of all this sacrifice is sacrificing our *dharma* to please the Lord of our life, Prananatha. Murari spoke about how the three modes control our nature, dictating us to act in a certain way.

He also enlightened Arjuna about the different *yoga* systems, delineating how the living entity connects with God, and ultimately, prescribing *bhakti yoga* as the topmost among all forms of *yoga*. Hence He asked Arjuna to surrender unto Him alone, abandoning all varieties of religions and isms, dovetailing them all for His cause. And what was Murari's cause? It was to establish the ultimate *dharma*, the *prema dharma* – the transcendental unmotivated and unalloyed loving service of the living entity unto the Supreme Lord Gopijana Vallabha.

Arjuna, whose illusion was dispelled by the grace of Hari's words, declared that he was pacified and would take up the fight. He was ready to strike with clarity, internally being aware as the non-doer, but externally acting with full attention.

As Arjuna heard the whole *Bhagavad Gita*, Yudhisthira Maharaja started walking towards the other side of the army. This caused great suspicion in the heart of all the Pandavas. They inquired with Nandanandana about this. He reassured them, saying, "I know why he is approaching them. He is performing his duty of seeking the blessings and permission of his superiors."

Yudhisthira seeked the blessings of Bhishma, Drona, Kripa and Shalya. Each one of them was compelled to offer him a benediction of being victorious. They said, "Yudhisthira, had you not come to us, we would have condemned you, but now we are pacified. You shall be victorious, because you have *dharma* on your side. We are simply bound by *artha*, we are servants of money, and hence we are fighting on behalf of Duryodhana. Though our weapons are for Duryodhana, our heartfelt blessings go out to you."

On the inspiration of Mukunda, Yudhisthira played another master stroke of standing between the two armies, and loudly proclaiming, "Now is the final chance, whoever wants to change their sides are welcome to do so, once the war begins then it is not possible to change." Yuyustava, Duryodhana's step-brother, promptly moved from Duryodhana's army to join the Pandavas' rank, causing a split in the Kuru forces and making their morale go down.

As Yudhisthira Maharaja was walking up to the Kauravas to seek their permission and blessings, Keshava, knowing that Karna wasn't going to fight as long as Bhishmadeva was alive, approached him with the intention of helping out the Pandavas. Being the Supreme Lord, He did not hesitate. As He had vowed to establish *dharma*, Keshava approached Karna without any reservation, although Karna was not in favour of *dharma*. If Karna could provide some service to the Pandavas even for a few days, Sri Krishna would be grateful. Shyamsundar wanted to give an opportunity to Karna to render service to the Pandavas, who were symbols of *dharma*. He asked him, "O Radheya! As long as Bhishmadeva is alive, you can battle on behalf of the Pandavas. Once he falls, then you return and fight for Duryodhana." But Karna denied the opportunity, "O Keshava! You must know that I am Duryodhana's well-wisher and willing to lay down my life for him. I refrain from doing anything that is not beneficial to him."

This is how Dinabandhu, by His own will, became an instrument in the hands of the Pandavas, even though everyone is an instrument in His hand. Out of kindness and affection, although He did not directly participate, He did impact the war as the time factor personified, whose mere glance had the power to minimize the life span of those who were opposed to *dharma*. Thus Purushottama was inconspicuously active on the battlefield by His mere glance. He had declared to Arjuna, "Become My instrument, and take all the glory."

No one other than Dinabandhu glorifies His own instruments, giving them the limelight. Who, in this world gives credit to those instrumental in their personal success? Yet He was simply driving Arjuna's chariot, giving them all the credit, and inundating the Pandavas by His unlimited affection and love.

chapter 16

DHARMA YUDDHA

As the war began, Bhishmadeva exhibited great valour and might, crushing the Pandavas' camp. By the end of day one, Shankha, the son of Virata was killed. Yudhisthira Maharaja became despondent, as he felt responsible for the death of his soldiers. He expressed his feelings to Madhusudana, saying that if he survived, he would go and perform *tapasya*. Yudhisthira Maharaja further asked Him, "What were the soldiers supposed to do? Arjuna despite being a great warrior was acting neutral, neither fighting nor using his *divyastra*. Only Bhima was fighting."

Govinda solaced Yudhisthira Maharaja saying, "Do not grieve, O Yudhisthira, it is not befitting you. Remember that your brothers are great heroes and that I am your well-wisher. I will do everything to ensure your victory. Satyaki, Virata, Drupada, and Drupada's son Dhrishtadyumna, these are all also great warriors who will devotedly fight on your behalf." In this way, Dwarkadhish was eternally there for Yudhisthira Maharaja. Each time he felt despondent, Hari would boost his confidence.

On day three, Bhishmadeva was still fighting gallantly, trouncing the Pandavas' army. Observing this, Keshava thought, "Arjuna is not fighting with his characteristic aggression and Bhishmadeva is about to destroy the entire army of the Pandavas. The soldiers are all fleeing in fear of Bhishma."

When Devakinandana was thus analyzing, Bhishma started shooting clusters of arrows at the chariot of Arjuna. All the warriors immediately scattered. Upon seeing all this, Sri Krishna declared to Satyaki, who was fighting with great valour, "O

Satyaki, let those who are running away leave and the remaining may stay. But I cannot trust them. Today, you shall witness the fate of Bhishma and Drona. No one in the army of the Kurus will be able to withstand My anger, nor will anyone leave the battle alive. Today, I will take away the life of Bhishma. O Satyaki! Today I shall kill Bhishma and Drona, and make Yudhisthira, Arjuna, Bhima, Nakula and Sahadeva fully satisfied. Today I shall kill the son of Dhritarashtra and establish Yudhisthira Maharaja as the king."

Saying this, Adideva remembered His *Sudarshana Chakra,* which instantly arrived. The all-powerful Parthasarathi, who could destroy the entire army, hurriedly unmounted His chariot and darted, His dazzling *pitambara* flapping in the wind, resembling a lightning bolt in the dark sky. His fury resembled the sun, and His beauty resembled a blooming lotus and His *Sudarshana Chakra* resembled the lotus petal. Shyamsundar was like an unlimited ocean and His divine form resembled a lotus stem.

As Devakinandana charged at Bhishmadeva wanting to destroy him, he remained composed and began to glorify, "O My Dear Lord, please come, O Deveshwara! O Jagata Niwas! I offer my obeisance unto You. Today, I accept Your shelter. In fact, the entire world is under Your shelter. My Lord, please annihilate me. If I die at Your hands, my destination in this world and the world beyond will be auspicious. O protector of the Andhakas and Vrishnis, by killing me, You will increase my glory in all the three worlds."

Seeing Hari enraged and about to kill Bhishmadeva, Arjuna hastily rushed to stop Him. His rage further inflamed as He saw Arjuna approaching. Just as a powerful tornado uproots many huge trees in its course, similarly Hari dragged Arjuna by His unstoppable force. Initially Arjuna could not stop Him from charging towards Bhishmadeva. Eventually, after mammoth effort, Arjuna could stall Mukunda by saying, "My dear Giridhari, I promise that I will carry out my duties, I will never give up my responsibilities. I vow in the name of my brothers and sons. By Your order, I will destroy the entire Kuru army."

Being assured thus, Parthasarathi became appeased and immediately returned to His chariot. Holding its reins, He drew the chariot further into the opposition side. Having experienced Sri Krishna's indignation, Arjuna shot a barrage of arrows at the great Kauravas who retired to their camps petrified. The entire night, they remained tensed about the gallant Arjuna. In this way, Purushottama was willing to break His own promise to protect the Pandavas. He also wanted to provoke & remind Arjuna of his duty. Janardhana's fiery reaction was intended to bring Arjuna back into action and make him fight the *dharma-yuddha* with his full might.

'Krishna' means all attractive; He who possess the magnetism to draw everyone closer to Him. He exhibited this aspect to Arjuna and Bhishmadeva. Hrishikesh drew Arjuna towards his duty and Bhishmadeva towards freedom from all his supposed obligations, duties and vows, which were, ironically, stumbling blocks to establishing *dharma*.

ARJUNA ATTACKS BHISHMADEVA

By day nine of the war, the mighty Bhishmadeva was still fighting ferociously, being provoked by Duryodhana. Padmanabha reminded Arjuna of his resolve to kill any warrior opposed to the Pandavas, including Bhishmadeva. He steered Arjuna, "If you are not enfeebled by attachment, the time is ripe to bring Bhishmadeva down. Be reminded what you vowed in the kingdom of Virata - to assault all the oppressors! Now, remember your *svadharma* and fight!"

These acute words of Sri Krishna bewildered the ferocious Arjuna, who hung his head low. He inquired, "My dear Purushottama, which will bring me more piety - killing our superiors for the attainment of kingdom or suffering in exile?" Arjuna was shaken at the thought of the ultimate confrontation with his beloved Bhishmadeva, which was now a reality. Parthasarathi maneuvered the chariot such that the arrows would not touch Arjuna. As the sun was setting, Bhishmadeva was demolishing the Pandavas' army, causing great impediment to his opponents.

Soon, Yadunatha was convinced that Arjuna was not fighting wholeheartedly, and the army of the Pandavas was feeling the heat of Bhishmadeva's might. Yadunatha could not tolerate this. He jumped off the chariot, broadening His shoulders, and as death personified, charged towards Bhishmadeva to execute him. Ghanashyam's dark complexion coupled with His effulgent attire resembled a thundering cloud racing forward. Bhishmadeva was least fearful noticing all this. He pleaded, "O Dinabandhu! Come and kill me! Deliver me! I am Your eternal servant. You can strike me as You desire."

Meanwhile, Arjuna rushed down to stop Yadunatha by grabbing His lotus feet, beseeching Him to spare Bhishmadeva. Arjuna reminded Achyuta of His own vow of not raising any weapon during the war and that if He killed Bhishmadeva, other warriors and people in general would disregard His word. Arjuna pleaded, promising to perform his duty ethically, having accepted the burden to fight. Devakinandana was glad to hear these words from His dear friend, but externally displayed anger and stomped off towards the chariot.

In spite of hearing the philosophy of *Gita*, it was unbearably painful for Arjuna to kill his own grandfather Bhishmadeva. Hence Nandakumar had to display His anger for two reasons - to rouse

Arjuna and bring him out of his attachment to Bhishmadeva, and to express His benevolence, "I am willing to break My vow of not raising any weapon to protect those who stand on the side of *dharma*".

NINTH NIGHT

In the Pandavas' camp, Yudhisthira was dejected seeing how the battle was progressing. Bhishmadeva's invincibility worried him. With a painful heart Yudhisthira spoke to Hari, "I will retire to the forest. I do not like this war, for my soldiers are getting killed. I am the cause of my brothers' suffering and anguish. While in the forest, Draupadi went through turmoil. My desire for kingdom is causing so much pain to everyone. Life is uncertain and for the rest of my time I would like to live in *dharma* by avoiding violence."

Damodara responded to the afflicted Yudhisthira compassionately, "Do not lament, your brothers are competent. If you order Me, I will kill Bhishmadeva. Once you order Me, why would I not fight? If you see victory only in killing Bhishmadeva, then certainly I will do that task. Pandavas' enemy is My enemy as well, there is no doubt in this regard. Your brother Arjuna is My dear friend, relative and disciple. For Arjuna, I can give My own flesh, and Arjuna can also sacrifice his very life for Me. It's our mutual vow to always help each other in difficulty. Arjuna has pledged to kill Bhishmadeva, now it is important that I fulfill it. It is not at all difficult for Arjuna to kill Bhishmadeva, as Arjuna and Bhima can destroy a host of *daityas* (demons) and *devatas* (demigods). Now, Bhishmadeva only has few days to live."

Simply by hearing the words of Hrishikesh, Yudhisthira Maharaja remembered the strategy to bring down Bhishmadeva. This was another kind of protection. Hari never used any weapon though He certainly promised to raise one if required. These words were sufficient enough to give the confidence and strategy to the extraordinary warriors, the Pandavas, to fight their enemies.

Showered with such inspiring and affectionate words, Yudhisthira Maharaja regained confidence. He expressed "My dear Shridhar, Your words certainly come true. What to speak of the Kauravas, even all *devatas* put together cannot bare Your power. With You on our side, Bhishmadeva is insignificant. But I cannot allow You to fight, for it will lead to You breaking Your vow. Providence has enlightened me the secret behind how Bhishmadeva could be killed."

Bhishmadeva himself had revealed the only way he could be killed. He had pledged to give up fighting if faced against any women or anyone resembling a woman. Otherwise Bhimsadeva was certainly invincible, even to his guru Parashurama, the warrior incarnation of the Lord. So the Pandavas, as advised by Bhishmadeva, placed Shikhandi, a woman in the previous birth, on Arjuna's chariot and the reluctant Arjuna by Parthasarathi's will and encouragement started attacking the great grandsire of the Kuru dynasty.

Arjuna, steeped in internal conflicts, faced great challenge in dealing with Bhishmadeva. Unlike the ruthless Duryodhana, who killed without hesitation, it was agonizing for the Pandavas to fight against those connected intimately, Bhishmadeva being the foremost. Arjuna loved him dearly. To overlook this affectionate relationship for the sake of establishing *dharma* was excruciatingly tough. Therefore, though Bhishmadeva was not an obstacle physically, even the thought of attacking him was unimaginable to Arjuna, even after hearing *Gita*.

Arjuna finally confessed this to Yadunatha, and although He empathized with him, Hari reminded Arjuna the fact of the matter that, sooner or later, Bhishmadeva's demise was inevitable. Having convinced him like this, Arjuna then achingly aimed at Bhishmadeva, piercing his body with multitudes of arrows, bringing him down to the ground. Thus Govinda protected the Pandavas by reinforcing them with strength in moments of weakness to carry out the inevitable.

Bhishmadeva was happy realizing that it was only Arjuna, whose arrows had the power to pierce his body. Thus Arjuna liberated Bhishmadeva from consistently being abused by the Kurus, albeit heavy-heartedly.

Before leaving his body, Bhishmadeva lay on a bed of arrows. This entire episode is beautifully described by Srila Vyasadeva in *Srimad Bhagavatam* and in the *Mahabharata* as well.

Parthasarathi guided, maneuvered, encouraged, provoked and instructed the Pandavas to stand and fight, simultaneously inspiring them to be conscious of Him and being sensitive of His energy.

FALL OF BHISHMADEVA

Janardhana then congratulated Yudhisthira Maharaja, saying, "You are gradually becoming victorious. Bhishmadeva was insurmountable even by all the demigods and demons put together. But your powerful glance, which can burn anyone to ashes, has indeed been effective." Relieved, Yudhisthira Maharaja responded, "I am convinced that victory will be ours since You have predicted it and we have taken Your shelter." Madhava simply nodded smilingly.

Thus the Lord always, without hesitation or pretence, gave all the credit to His devotees. This quality of Bhaktavatsala Sri Krishna made Him dearer to the Pandavas, who were already completely enamoured by Him. With an unassuming nature, Dinabandhu was always eager to serve the Pandavas wholeheartedly, but never accepted credit, always passing it on to the Pandavas.

VALOUR, FAITH & VOW

Whenever Sanjaya narrated about the fate of the Kauravas to the Kuru King, he glorified Nandanandana and concluded by describing His power and supremacy. But interestingly, this time, Dhritarashtra glorified Hari after the fall of Bhishmadeva. He recited several pastimes of Yashodanandana killing many demons and vanquishing many so-called kings during Rukmini's marriage ceremony

Dhritarashtra said, "Arjuna is the soul of Sri Krishna, and Sri Krishna is Arjuna's soul. Victory always resides in Arjuna and fame is inconsequential for Brajanatha. Duryodhana is ignorant for he does not know that these two are the eternal Nara and Narayana. They are one soul in two different bodies. One cannot even defeat them in one's own mind. Simply by their will, they can annihilate my entire army, but they are acting as though they are ordinary humans."

ARJUNA PROTECTED FROM VAISHNAVASTRA

Bhagadatta, the great grandsire of the Kuru clan, was a warrior of great stature. On the battlefield, the epic day arrived where Bhagadatta was to fight Arjuna. A fierce battle ensued between the two. During its course, Bhagadatta fired an infallible weapon called *Vaishnavastra* at Arjuna, which the Lord of the milk ocean had benedicted Bhagadatta with. However Arjuna was saved from the jaws of death by the timely intervention of Dinanatha. As the weapon speedily darted to sever Arjuna's head, Keshava stood between the arrow and Arjuna. To everyone's astonishment that very weapon turned into a beautiful *Vaijayanti* garland, which always adorns Lord Vishnu.

The perturbed Arjuna questioned Yadunatha, "Why did You break Your promise? You were not supposed to defend or fight, but only be my charioteer. It is one thing to protect me when I am in danger, but I am a vigilant and accomplished fighter. All the demigods together cannot defeat me, why did You defend me then?"

Madanmohan explained the secret of the *Vaishnavastra* weapon to Arjuna, "I expand into four forms. My first form resides in Badrinatha as Nara and Narayana. My second form resides as *Paramatma* (the super soul) in everyone's heart. My third form is present in this world in the human feature. And My fourth form resides in the causal ocean. Once Bhumidevi asked a benediction for her son in the form of this weapon. I delivered the weapon to her son Narakasura, who was eventually killed by Me. Then the *Vaishanavastra* was handed over to Bhagadatta. I am fully aware of its implications. Unstoppable that the weapon is, no power in this world can reduce its speed. But the weapon is completely under My control. O Arjuna! I had to intervene in order to protect you. Now is the time to kill Bhagadatta and his elephant."

Since Bhagadatta was old, he would tie a cloth on his forehead in order to keep the eyelids open. The Supreme Knower, Janardhana, instructed Arjuna to cut off that cloth so that Bhagadatta could not see anything. Soon, Bhagadatta was defeated by Arjuna. Thus Arjuna easily killed both, Bhagadatta and his elephant.

In the battle of Mahabharata, the Pandavas were certainly blessed. But the Kuru dynasty also had its own share of gallant warriors with endless, formidable benedictions. It was humanly impossible to make each benediction go in vain. But Adideva was the source of all the benedictions and also of reversing those benedictions which were being used against the cause of religion.

Bhishmadeva had the weapon called *Iccha Mrityu* (death by one's own will), Drona could kill by weapons and by words, Karna had the domineering *Shakti* weapon, Ashwathama had the ultimate *Narayanastra*, and he could not be killed and Bhagadatta had *Vaishnavastra*. But Hari cleverly rendered each of them impotent and Arjuna did the rest to bring them down once they were stripped of their divine benedictions by Mukunda.

SUMMARY OF THE CHAKRAVYUHA

On the Pandavas' side only Mathuresh Krishna, Arjuna, Pradyumna and Abhimanyu knew the art of breaking into the seven-tier defensive spiral formation known as the *Chakravyuha*. But Abhimanyu did not know the way to exit that *Chakravyuha*. Drona, with the intention of putting the Pandavas army in great danger had master-minded this formation. Drona engaged Arjuna in fighting the Trigaratha brothers, who had vowed of not returning from the battle unless they took Arjuna's life. So Arjuna was forced to accept their challenge and Devakinandana agreed to this proposal.

When Abhimanyu was informed about the predicament, he immediately volunteered to assist. Yudhisthira was completely unwilling. But the persistent and confident Abhimanyu hoping once the formation was broken into, it would open the gates for the great Pandava warriors headed by Bhima to enter in, eventually convinced Yudhisthira, who hesitantly agreed. But Abhimanyu's confidence proved too fatal, taking his own life. Jayadratha, much to their dismay, intervened and successfully stopped the Pandavas from entering the *Chakravyuha*.

Jayadratha was the brother-in-law of Duryodhana who had

previously attempted to molest Draupadi during her exile in the forest with the Pandavas, and when the Pandavas, especially Bhima were punishing him, Yudhisthira being kind-hearted restrained Bhima from killing him.

Rather than feeling grateful for being forgiven, Jayadratha decided to avenge his insult by the Pandavas and rigorously began worshipping Lord Shiva, who rejected Jayadratha's desire for a benediction of being able to kill the Pandavas. Instead Lord Shiva give a benediction to defeat the Pandavas, except Arjuna, once in his life, and this was the fateful day Jayadratha chose.

Abhimanyu fought single-handedly and defeated the great Karna and Drona, but eventually they all attacked the lone fighter Abhimanyu like owls. He died a glorious death, and his killers survived, only to be condemned for their cowardly act forever. The celestial living beings used this gruesome incident to demonstrate that even animals were sensitive, but humans had lost their sensitivity and became less than four-legged animals and birds.

DEATH OF ABHIMANYU

Undoubtedly, this episode -'The glorious death of Abhimanyu', is most gruesome and painful. Even the kind-hearted become enraged. Only the ruthless remain unaffected.

This incident usually raises some questions - How could Abhimanyu, the dearmost nephew of Janardhana meet this fate? Why didn't Sri Krishna protect him? How could Abhimanyu be so brutally murdered? All these doubts, lead one to question the very Godhood of Sri Krishna.

The answer lies in the very foundational understanding of the scriptures. Absolute knowledge is not limited to and hence can't be deciphered on the basis of our limited, relative experiences of this world. Our experiences are steeped in dualities. Our conviction is based on the limited horizon of our experiences, culture and immediate environment. These alone do not constitute an infallible wisdom bank. Such inferences are simply based on a series of events. Though our experiences are real, they do not constitute as absolute, especially when they are seen through the lens of bias and prejudice.

The only way to understand the knowledge of the absolute is through the eyes of the scriptures, the lens of *dharma*, which, being given by God, are infallible with respect to past, present and future. This is the only true way to gauge the happenings of our relative world.

What actually is *dharma*? *Dharma* is governance by cosmic law. It is neither man-made nor micro-managed by God. However it acts under the supervision and empowerment of God. Material nature works independently, not by rebelling against God but by being under His superintendence, just as the Mayor does not control the water department by his personal daily supervision. The department works independent of the intervention of the Mayor, though created by him. Similarly, God does not get involved in the management of this phenomenal material world, on a day-to-day basis.

Through the death of Abhimanyu, Hari enables the Pandavas, and more so the readers, to experience the 'human' side of this world, through the reality check of dualities like pain and pleasure, victory and defeat, living and dying, selfishness and self-sacrifice, evil and good, sickness and health, attachment and indifference. This aspect forms the very core principle of this world. Even though the Pandavas did not belong to this world, they submitted to the laws of this world and Hari certainly allowed this principle to operate.

In the beginning of the *Bhagavad Gita*, Keshava did not give Arjuna an assurance of victory, but rather asked Arjuna to perform his duty of fighting as a *kshatriya*, irrespective of the outcome. Being duty bound is the very essence of the knowledge of *Gita*. We have duties on the level of body and soul. This is the concept of *Nishkama Karma yoga*. This is the *yoga* of action without expectation. It is duty bound *yoga*, and duty itself becomes the reward.

Abhimanyu was only performing his duty and not expecting Damodara to protect him. In fact for Abhimanyu this attitude was Hari's way of protecting him. He became a hero for a higher cause, for the cause of becoming a selfless instrument of Hari in establishing *dharma* by sacrificing his very life. Abhimanyu was most happy to do so to aid the Lord's cause, his consciousness was free from any expectations that Hari would come and protect him physically. Instead Abhimanyu concluded that this was how his life would be utilized in Hari's service. This understanding of Abhimanyu and devotees like Abhimanyu is one of the most important protections of the Lord. This understanding never makes them raise a question about Hari's involvement in their lives.

Therefore Abhimanyu was proud to fight like a hero. He was caught in a whirlwind of the Kauravas' army, headed by Drona, who had formed the *Chakravyuha*. Abhimanyu was expert at entering the whirlwind but untrained to come out of it. He was forced by the circumstances to defend himself knowing the stakes were very high.

He neither regretted his decision of entering the *chakra* nor complained the lack of support he experienced. He never blamed Govinda for not offering him protection, rather the gallant young warrior only focused on letting his uncle Sri Krishna and father Arjuna know that he chivalrously fought the war which would eternally make them proud. Anyone who reads this episode of Mahabharata would at least be inspired to walk in the footsteps of the gutsy warrior Abhimanyu and to live and die like him.

Yadunatha consoled the Pandavas on the loss of the heroic Abhimanyu. Though they were attached to him, they never gave up their duty of fighting for *dharma*. This was the protection they received from Yadunatha. Conversely we see that Drona stopped fighting on hearing the news of his son's death. Thus Drona's cause for participating in the battle was insignificant. Arjuna, on the other hand, who had also lost his son never held himself back from fighting. Though his heart was in despair and indescribable gloom persisted, nevertheless he remained fixed in his mission, and continued to destroy the Kuru army. With the death of Abhimanyu, Arjuna transformed his internal turmoil into crystal clear vision as he realized that he was fighting for the sake of Sri Krishna and *dharma*, and despair could not dissuade him from fighting.

With Abhimanyu's glorious death, it is relevant to mention the dialogue between the demigods and the Moon God, the original father of Abhimanyu. The demigods, including Abhimanyu, had descended on earth to assist the Lord's incarnation in establishing *dharma*, but it was the desire of Moon God that his son, Abhimanyu, shall not remain on earth for long and must return to him as early as possible. Thus, as destined, Abhimanyu departed young but not without putting a great fight, and although short-lived, the impact was long lasting. Certainly the desire of Moon God was fulfilled.

ARJUNA VOWS TO KILL JAYADRATHA

On being informed how Abhimanyu was ruthlessly attacked and killed, Arjuna was greatly infuriated and pained, feeling intense separation from his son. His eternal loving well-wishers Yudhisthira and Mukunda, while desolate and grieving themselves, gently consoled Arjuna.

Yudhisthira narrated the details of the merciless incident to Arjuna and upon hearing of Jayadratha's involvement in stopping other Pandavas from entering into the *chakra* formation, the enraged Arjuna resolved to attack Jayadaratha. He vowed, "If I don't slay him tomorrow before the sun sets, I will jump into fire. Only if he takes shelter of my Yudhisthira and Sri Krishna, I shall forgive and not kill him." Even in that emotional outburst, Arjuna was very careful to consider in which condition to spare someone who was party to his son's death.

SRI KRISHNA'S ANXEITY OVER ARJUNA'S VOW AND IT'S FULFILLMENT

Madhusudana was peeved by Arjuna's spontaneous vow. The Lord questioned Arjuna how he could boldly declare a vow without duly consulting his seniors. Arjuna modestly reminded Madhusudana of his valour and skills and expressed that he got strength knowing He would be on his side. With gratitude, Arjuna said, "If I have Your grace, no power in the world can stop me. Just as a real *brahmana* is always truthful, a saint is always humble, and Laxmi is present in every *yagya*, similarly wherever Lord Narayana resides, victory is certain."

Pundarikasha tried to console His grieving sister Subhadra, Abhimanyu's wife Uttara and Draupadi. The ladies were going through such a whirlwind of emotions that He was perplexed trying to solace them. Still, the duty bound Lord fulfilled His obligation and tried consoling them.

The soldiers were so anxious hearing the vow that while praying for Arjuna's success, they did not even rest that night. Although they knew the dignity and power of Arjuna, they prayed for

85

the Lord's blessings upon him and that their own pious credits be bestowed upon him, so that he could be victorious over Jayadratha.

Meanwhile, Mukunda awoke in the middle of the night, and ordered His charioteer Daruka, "O Daruka! Arjuna has taken this terrible vow, and Duryodhana certainly would want Arjuna to fail at any cost so that he can jump in the fire. With Dronacharya on Duryodhana's side, even Indra cannot defeat him. Therefore I have decided to do something to ensure that Arjuna can kill Jayadratha before the sun sets tomorrow. Keep my weapons ready. Arjuna is dearer to Me than all My wives, family and everyone I know put together. I cannot live without him. I cannot imagine any harm being inflicted upon him. One who hates Arjuna, verily hates Me! One who follows him, follows Me! Tomorrow when I blow My conch in the *Rishabha* note, then you may proceed to the battlefield so that I can eliminate all the Kuru warriors and protect My Arjuna's vow."

That night, Arjuna, while meditating on Lord Shiva through the mantra given by Srila Vyasadeva, fell asleep. He had a dream – Devakinandana visited Arjuna and he offered Him a place to sit. He conversed with Arjuna and assured him of success, and then took him along to Lord Shiva's planet. There, Arjuna was benedicted with the *Pashupata astra* again.

This dream infused Arjuna with the confidence to win. Yudhisthira Maharaja also prayed to Purushottama while glorifying Him. Krishnachandra assured Yudhisthira Maharaja about Arjuna's victory.

The next day, Arjuna was fighting fiercely. Drona approached Arjuna to battle, but Achyuta strategically reminded Arjuna that battling Drona at this point was a useless waste of time as the priority was to kill Jayadratha before the sun sets. Arjuna immediately circumambulated his guru, Drona, and started to proceed. To this Drona objected, condemning him saying, "A real warrior never runs away from his enemy." Arjuna responded, "You are my guru, not my enemy. You are undefeatable". Dinabandhu was committed to protect Arjuna's vow.

As Arjuna was proceeding at the speed of mind, his chariot was expertly maneuvered by Parthasarathi. At one point of time, Arjuna's horses were tired. To everyone's amazement, releasing the horses, Parthasarathi Himself began feeding and nursing them. Arjuna immediately manifested a beautiful water lake. Yadunatha lovingly served the horses, feeding them, giving them water and massaging them. The rejuvenated horses tried licking Gopala, reminding everyone of His cow herding pastimes in Vrindavana.

As Vrajamohan was tending the horses, Arjuna disembarked his chariot and the warriors could have easily targeted to kill him. Yet, everyone was so enamoured by Govinda's charming ways that no opponent could harm Arjuna. It was as though Govinda's charm extended an armour-like protection for Arjuna. Arjuna was fighting the soldiers, and even though he was off his chariot, Arjuna did not plead them not to shoot at him. It was a mesmerizing combination of Madanmohan's charming beauty and Arjuna's charming dexterity and confidence.

DEATH OF BHURISHRAVA

Going forward, Arjuna had to deal with Bhurishrava, a gallant warrior fighting on behalf of the Kurus, who was about to kill Satyaki. Satyaki was Yogeshwara's cousin and Arjuna's disciple. Seeing Satyaki in danger, Sri Krishna prompted Arjuna's intervention, and Arjuna dexterously cut off Bhurishrava's limb with his sharp arrows. Bhurishrava condemned Arjuna, "You would not have been able to kill me unless you were provoked

87

by Yogeshwara Krishna". Arjuna responded "It is the duty of a warrior and especially a king to protect those who are protecting him. Satyaki was protecting me so it was my duty to protect him".

By alerting Arjuna, Dayanidhi protected his sense of duty towards his subordinates. It is unfair for the subordinate warriors to lay their lives for the protection of their leader when the leader can't protect them at the cost of risking his own life when needed. Arjuna reiterated this to Bhurishrava, who condemned Murari and Arjuna for causing this war.

In reality, Bhurishrava was an ardent worshiper of Lord Vishnu, and the original Vishnu, Sri Krishna, was right in front of him. Mukunda did punish Bhurishrava but keeping his ultimate good in mind. Bhurishrava was sent to Vaikuntha, the planet of no contamination and no return.

The extent of Dinabandhu's reward is always higher than the apparent punishment. Here, He reinstates the fact that the act of punishment is not necessarily cruel, it depends on the intention of the authority. If the leader's intention is to benefit the offender, then the person so punished can actually benefit. Of course, one cannot imitate Sri Krishna's supreme authority to decide whom and how to punish.

DEATH OF JAYADRATHA

While Arjuna fought fiercely, the sun was about to set. Realizing the call of the hour, Mukunda tipped Arjuna that he could not make it to Jayadratha, who was protected by six *maharathis* or stalwart warriors on all sides, without the aid of *maya* or illusion. Hence, Ajitatma recommended, "I will create an illusion of darkness such that only Jayadratha will perceive as though the sun is setting. Thus, eager to witness your death, he will come out in the open. Seizing this opportunity, knowing that the sun has not already set, you should cut off Jayadratha's head." Arjuna was satisfied to hear the plot.

Yogeshwara, the master of all mystic *yoga*, then covered the battlefield with a curtain of darkness, while the sun was still up. Jayadratha joyously comprehended that the sun was setting, but still Arjuna continued to fight for a while.

Yogeshwara, aware of a benediction that Jayadratha's father Vridhaksatra was awarded, that whoever makes his son's head roll on the ground would be reduced to splinters instantly, ordered Arjuna to behead Jayadratha in such a manner that his head falls in the lap of his own father.

Thus, Arjuna following His instructions with great precision, severed Jayadratha's head such that it travelled the distance and fell upon his father's lap. Vridhaksatra, feeling something fall on his lap while performing his evening oblations, instinctively jerked, making his son's head roll off to the ground, thus becoming the victim of his own curse and his own head reduced to splinters.

Thus, in this incident, Madhusudana's protection to Arjuna was two-fold: protection from upholding his vow of killing Jayadratha before sunset and thus from having him to enter the fire, and secondly, from death by the curse of Vridhaksatra.

Had it not been for Yadunatha's protection, then either ways, Arjuna would have been killed by end of that day, whether he killed Jayadratha or not. This would have surely been a win-win situation for the Kauravas, who did not mind staking Jayadratha, as long as the formidable Arjuna was out of the picture for good. But Duryodhana and his party failed to realize, that with Ajita on the Pandavas side, who had vowed to protect them under all circumstances, victory for the Kurus was impossible.

Witnessing supreme shelter under Achyuta's unfailing protection, from this day onwards, Arjuna was completely transformed. He was now wholeheartedly committed to fight and assist Him in establishing *dharma* on the planet.

Mukunda heartily congratulated Arjuna, saying, "O Arjuna! Successfully carrying out such a herculean task is only possible for you! Even the entire army of the demigods would have perished while facing the Kauravas."

With deep gratitude, Arjuna replied, glorifying Keshava, "For those who are under Your protection, victory is certain. By Your influence, we will always remain the objects of Your felicitations." Arjuna was modest and practical, yet he found the sound of Hari's compliments sweeter than nectar as it revealed His loving affection unto the Pandavas.

chapter 18
GHATOTHKACH BECOMES THE PAWN

As the battle progressed, one day Arjuna desired to confront Karna face to face. But Dwarkadhish stopped him. The Pandavas were not only fortunate to be able to discuss everything with Him, but also had the innate quality of accepting His proposed direction after duly contemplating its value. Even though they had unwavering faith, they never accepted or rejected any suggestion blindly.

Shyamsundar explained to Arjuna, "I do not consider your encounter with Karna is required. There are only two individuals who can confront Karna, you and Ghatothkach. Karna has the *Shakti* weapon to strike you, so let us summon Ghatothkach." Murari called him and instructed him to destroy the Kuru army, especially Karna. Ghatothkach, the son of Bhima and the demoness Hidimbi, willingly accepted and was ready to strike.

This was a brilliant strategy orchestrated by Madhava, who wanted to force Karna to use up the *Shakti* weapon to tackle Ghatothkach, who could not be killed by any ordinary weapon. And once Karna had used his trump card - the *Shakti* weapon, it meant an unobstructed path of victory for Arjuna. Simultaneously, Janardhana wanted Ghatothkach, being a demon and hence against the culture of *dharma*, to die. Duryodhana's army was soon being destroyed by Ghatothkach's strength and Karna had no choice but to use the *Shakti* weapon to finish him. Thus, Madhava was shrewd and one-pointed in His strategy. Ghatothkach had to perish and the *Shakti* weapon had to be usurped. Karna's death would simply be a consequence of all this.

Now, Karna intuitively knew that his own destruction was close, and Hari wanted him defeated. Ghatothkach's great fortune was that Hari engaged his demoniac propensity in service, albeit at the cost of his very life.

In this way, Nandakumar protected the religious Pandavas by using another *upapandava*, the son of the Pandava, Ghatothkach, as a sacrificial lamb, and gave him the credit for being a great warrior.

KRISHNA CELEBRATES DEATH OF GHATOTHKACH

Devakinandana was happy on the death of Ghatothkach but the Pandavas were in extreme pain although he died gloriously.

Inquisitive Arjuna questioned Damodara the cause of His happiness, to which the Supreme Intelligent explained, "O great Arjuna! Today Indra's *Shakti* weapon was used up by Karna, now your defeating him is assured. Who had the courage and power to handle Karna with his *Shakti* weapon? It is our good fortune that he has lost his armour, earring and now the *Shakti* weapon. Karna certainly was undefeatable with these attributes. He was unmatchable even with My *Sudarshana* and your *Gandiva*. Now he is as good as an ordinary warrior. I killed Jarasandha and Ekalavya for your benefit. If Chediraja Shishupala, Ekalavya, Karna and Jarasandha had to join forces with Duryodhana, the Kurus would have been invincible. To establish *dharma*, I killed those opposed to it. I declare unto you Arjuna! Wherever *Veda*, truthfulness, *dharma*, shyness and forgiveness exist, I reside there happily."

These enlightening words kept Arjuna humble and diligent. Madhusudana could have effortlessly killed countless Karnas and Jarasandhas. But He acted on the human-like platform, thus humbling Arjuna as well. Arjuna never took credit for his triumphs either.

Murari was removing so many demons from the surface of the earth so that the job of the Pandavas became easy. Why was He favouring them? Because the Pandavas were righteous, receptive and without any personal agenda. In fact, they wished to renounce, or live by ruling over just five villages. What to speak of the other Pandavas, even the belligerent Bhima was willing to live with less. The purpose of this war was to fulfill the Lord's desire to establish *dharma* and wipe out the irreligious Kurus. Hence the Pandavas, with great reluctance and not out of personal choice, were willing to rule on behalf of Jagannatha.

Damodara certainly protected Arjuna from the mighty warriors, but importantly, He protected his sense of benevolence and humility. Without these qualities, men are no better than beasts, because power degrades a human to levels worst than a brutal beast.

WHY KARNA DID NOT RELEASE SHAKTI ON ARJUNA

Often this question is raised as to why Karna did not attack Arjuna with his *Shakti* weapon to kill him on the very first day of the battle. Obviously, that would have ended the war easily. Dhritarashtra inquired from Sanjaya, on hearing about the death of Ghatothkach, "Arjuna's death would have spelt doom for the Pandavas. Arjuna had the resolute vow of never abandoning the battlefield. So shouldn't Karna have looked for killing Arjuna first?"

Sanjaya answered, quoting that the same question was raised by Satyaki to Madhusudana, who replied to Satyaki, "Each day after the battle, back in the Kurus' camp, Duryodhana, Shakuni and

Dushasana would urge Karna to kill Arjuna, and Karna, who was very much determined to do so, would agree, but every day on the battlefield, I was bewildering Karna's intelligence, so that he would not attack as per his resolve. Protecting Arjuna was more important than protecting my father, mother, brothers like you and even Myself."

Such protection is out of Lord's compassion and affection and not in the physical sphere per se. Physically, it was not possible for anyone to harm Arjuna by any means. When Adideva, the source of everything that exists advents to this world, He combines His *sarvagyata* (omniscience) with *mugdhata* (incognizance), under the auspices of His internal potency *Yogamaya*. This enables Him to experience the sweetness of human-like pastimes, which gives rise to feelings like anxiety, fear and affection towards someone who is intimately connected with Him, like the devout Arjuna. Hence such protection sprang from deep affection.

chapter 19
CLASH BETWEEN LIE & DHARMA

This is a story which is largely susceptible to being miscomprehended by many. How could Achyuta suggest to Yudhisthira, the personification of truth, to lie for a mere kingdom at the cost of disregarding his virtue?

Drona was teacher of the Kurus and Angirasa's student. He had received divine weapons from Parashurama and had the indomitable power to kill by weapons as well as by curse. *Sapada api* or *Sharada api* - curse or weapons. But how does his death - a conspiracy of his own students against him under the strategic lead of Dwarkadhish - demonstrate protection of *dharma*?

This portion of the episode depicts the Lord's actions for the cause of *dharma*.

Purushottama, observing that Drona had already killed Virata and Drupada and was still fighting fiercely, realized that he was insurmountable. The Lord informed Yudhisthira that unless Drona was stalled, his entire army would be destroyed.

One way to stop him was to falsely inform him that his son, Ashwathama was dead. Arjuna initially disliked this ploy and *Dharmaraja* Yudhisthira was hesitant, but they realized the gravity of Drona annihilating their soldiers in multitudes and that, by fair means or foul, he had to be checked, otherwise the battle would be a lost cause. It was a known fact that Drona was fighting for the pleasure of his beloved son, who shared friendship with Duryodhana. So Yudhisthira Maharaja reluctantly agreed and Bhima immediately killed an elephant named Ashwathama.

Drona was informed of the death of Ashwathama, yet he

continued to fight fiercely. Then the *rishis* approached Drona, telling him to withdraw and leave his body, but he still continued unabated. Yadunatha then exhorted Yudhisthira to either lie to Drona or lose the war as Drona would not believe anyone else. Then Yudhisthira informed Drona that Ashwathama is killed, yet murmured "the elephant" under his breath. These words from Yudhisthira, the adherent of truth, mortified Drona, yet he continued his war with Dhristadyumna. This made Bhima furious and he spoke rudely, "O *brahmana*! What are you doing? Even after your son is dead, you are still fighting! You have given up your *dharma* and are killing people like a butcher!!" Eventually, the despondent Drona fainted, dropping his weapons, and recited the Omkar while remembering Sri Narayana.

Purushottama, Arjuna, Yudhisthira, Kripacharya and Sanjaya saw Drona's soul enter Brahmaloka to search for his son's soul. Dhrishtadyumna, seizing the opportunity, grabbed Drona's hair and beheaded him. Arjuna tried hard to stop Dhrishtadyumna from beheading Drona, but it was in vain. Dhrishtadyumna was born to kill Drona. He severed his head and threw it towards Duryodhana. Such was the ghastly death of Drona at the hands of the Pandava army.

Mukunda had no choice but to finish Drona as he showed no sign of slowing down; he was inhumanly slaying the opposition, losing his inherent *brahminical* sensitivity. He was invincible and only the weapon of deceit could stop him, especially coming from Yudhisthira, the very emblem of truthfulness. Thus Yudhisthira spoke the famous lie, which will forever remain imprinted in the hearts of the readers of *Mahabharata*.

For Yudhisthira, it was a great predicament between personal ethic and the cause of *dharma*. Abiding by his personal *dharma* may have been satisfying for his own conscience, but the larger cause, the universal *dharma*, called for establishing a *dharmik*

96

kingdom. Yudhisthira chose to 'lie', albeit reluctantly, as he was duty bound and not out of personal weakness. Thus Janardhana protected Yudhisthira by helping him to befittingly discriminate between universal *dharma* over personal *dharma*, by prioritizing the benefit of humanity at large.

Those who understand the nuances of *dharma* see the instruction of Hrishikesh to lie and the universal principle of *dharma* with the same vision. Often the righteous are sneered at by the *adharmik* saying, "How can you, who are so virtuous, adopt unethical means, playing the same game as us?" Seeing 'ethics' as a water-tight set of rules, they insist that *dharmik* people strictly abide by the letter of *dharma*, irrespective of the end result, while the rest can enjoy under the label of '*adharma*', exploiting *dharma* for the wrong reason.

The Pandavas could never have conceived of this plot. Yogeshwara tactically did the needful for a higher cause, keeping in mind the long-term welfare of society. As was His style, He only suggested the idea, opening up the options before the Pandavas. It could be seen as a choice between two evils – letting Drona survive versus killing him. While the latter involved personal *adharma* for Yudhisthira, the former had far-reaching implications: the colossal violence caused by Drona leading to the downfall of the Pandavas, eventually making the iniquitous Duryodhana emporer of the world. This would fundamentally foil the reason why the war was being fought - to check Duryodhana's hedonistic autocracy.

With Parthasarathi's judicious guidance, the Pandavas were protected from superficially practicing *dharma*, thereby causing *adharma* to rule. The very essence of *dharma* would have been lost! Externally, it may appear that the Pandavas did not fight virtuously, but the end-motive of fighting was to establish a kingdom of virtue.

ASHWATHAMA AND NARAYANASTRA

When Ashwathama discovered about Yudhisthira's treachery and his father's humiliating death at the hands of Dhrishtadyumna, he declared to Duryodhana that he would release the insurmountable *Narayanastra*, which, being given to Dronacharya personally by Lord Narayana, was in turn passed on to him. Ashwathama proclaimed, "No one has this weapon - neither Devakinandana nor Arjuna. And their defeat is now certain."

As soon as Ashwathama released the weapon, the Pandava army was shattered. Yudhisthira became morose, condemning himself, and Arjuna deplored Yudhisthira for his deceitfulness to gain a kingdom. An argument broke out between Bhima and Arjuna. Dhrishtadyumna being distressed almost attacked Arjuna. Satyaki, who shielded Arjuna, condemned Dhrishtadyumna for killing Dronacharya. Finally, Madhava and Yudhisthira somehow pacified the Pandavas. Thus, even after his demise, Drona caused conflict in the Pandava army.

The all-knowing Achyuta, signalled everyone in the Pandava army to disembark their chariots, horses and elephants. He ordered those on the ground to fold their hands and not retaliate the *Narayanastra*, even mentally. If it was defended, the *Narayanastra* would even go to the lower planets and kill the enemy. Everyone, but Bhima, instantly complied. Bhima, who was the only one persistently fighting Ashwathama, admonished Arjuna saying, "How could you put your *Gandiva* down? This will bring you eternal infamy." Arjuna promptly responded, "I have no hesitation in withdrawing from the *Narayanastra, brahmanas* and cows."

Bhima kept fighting but the weapon, blazing like a giant planet, was invincible. Arjuna released *Varunastra* to protect Bhima, and both Arjuna and Damodara rushed towards Bhima, forcing him to descend his chariot. Karunasindhu informed Bhima, "If by fighting we could win against the Kurus, we would be doing that, but at this moment, we can only succeed by throwing our weapons," Bhima relented and came down. Immediately, the *Narayana* weapon became passive and harmony prevailed.

Thus the Pandavas' army was protected, simply by offering obeisances to the weapon. Seeing this, Duryodhana guessed that the Pandava army was ready to fight back so he urged Ashwathama to release the *Narayanastra* again. But the son of Drona said, "It is impossible. It can only be released once, and if tried again it will destroy its source."

Ashwathama had the satisfaction of making the Pandavas bow down, but Mukunda had the satisfaction of protecting the Pandavas in an exclusive way, by feigning disability to the divine weapon. But Duryodhana was dissatisfied seeing them alive. He was not interested to see the Pandavas lose their dignity by bowing down, he just wanted them finished.

Hrishikesh taught the Pandavas a practical lesson in surrendering. It is fruitless to fight for a cause, which is beyond one's capability. Once they were free from the hazard, the Pandavas were ready to strike back by performing their *svadharma* of fighting like Kshatriyas.

Ashwathama, distraught to see his weapon fail, confessed to Srila Vyasadeva about his predicament. Vyasadeva, revealed to Ashwathama the identity of Sri Krishna, whose very weapon was the *Narayanastra*, so how could it possibly hurt its owner and His devotees?

chapter 20

CONCERN BECOMES CONFLICT

After Drona's demise, the Kauravas were fast heading towards their ill fate, with defeat and death looming larger with each warrior's fall. Duryodhana had lost almost all of his brothers and relatives. Duryodhana, who had great confidence in his bosom friend Karna, decided to install him as his commander-in-chief, although he was bereft of his might in the absence of his special armour, earring, and *Shakti* weapon. Besides this, the curses of Parashurama and the *brahmana* would also effectuate, as Karna was to face his most difficult enemy towards the culmination of the battle.

SRI KRISHNA, THE MEDIATOR

This is a very dramatic, captivating and illuminating tale of how Purushottama mediated between Yudhisthira and Arjuna. It evinces different facets of imprudence exhibited by people and how an expert mediator deals with them, helping to bring out a symbiotic and harmonious outcome with least damage.

Ever since the undaunted Karna vowed to kill Arjuna, Yudhisthira was always anxious about Arjuna's protection and the subsequent plan of their rightful kingdom. It was a known fact to one and all that Karna was the biggest hope for Duryodhana and the greatest fear for the Pandavas.

The newly appointed commander-in-chief of the Kurus, Karna wreaked havoc in the Pandava camp, as if it was hit by a tornado. Karna brutally wounded and humiliated Yudhisthira, who, bleeding and offended, came to the army camp for medical aid.

Meanwhile, Arjuna, not noticing his brother's flag on the battlefield, requested Bhima to lead the army, while he tried searching for him, worried that he may have died. Parthasarathi drew his chariot and brought Arjuna to the camp. When Yudhisthira saw Sri Krishna and Arjuna, he assumed with great expectation that their arrival heralded the good news of Karna's death, without them being personally harmed. Hence Yudhisthira eagerly awaited all the details of Arjuna slaying Karna, who was a nightmare for Yudhisthira for all these years.

Instead, Arjuna distressed Yudhisthira, outlining how Karna was very much alive and causing havoc on the battlefield, pulverizing powerful warriors. But at the same time, Arjuna assured Yudhisthira, promising him to kill Karna, with his due blessings.

Hearing all this, Yudhisthira became furious and spoke harshly with Arjuna. He had never insulted anybody in his entire life. It was worse than the lie which he spoke during the war with Drona in the eyes of *dharma*. Many readers of *Mahabharata* are not privy to this episode.

Yudhisthira condemned Arjuna, "You are a coward. You ran away from the battlefield, leaving Bhima alone to his fate. You had taken a vow in Dwaitavana, saying you would kill Karna but now here you are, fearful of facing him. If you were not able to kill him, why the hell did you ignite this fire of death with such massive loss of life? You had promised us many fruits, but you are a fruitless tree, causing mere disappointment. Duryodhana had proclaimed that Arjuna couldn't stand Karna's gallantry on the battlefield. How foolish I was to believe otherwise! O Yadunatha! I gathered so many warriors to fight on my behalf, but see the conclusion? Now I can only depend on Bhima, who is fighting alone on the battlefield."

Yudhisthira continued, "O Partha! If Abhimanyu was alive today, I would not be in this position and also if Ghatothkach was living then the picture would be different. Better give your *Gandiva* to Sri Krishna, and be the charioteer instead. Either you should have fallen from the womb of our mother during her fifth month, or you should not have entered her womb in the first place! At least that way, we would have never entered this war."

The king continued, giving a final blow which broke Arjuna, inciting him to kill his own elder brother, for whose sake he tolerated all the offenses against Draupadi in the assembly of the Kurus, and for whom he was fighting this very war. "Your *Gandiva* is useless and so are your powerful shoulders which are apparently known for their valour. Your unlimited weapons and your flag which is being duly neglected by Hanuman, and your chariot which is offered by Agnideva, all these put together are of no use."

While Shridhara sympathized with Yudhisthira, Arjuna was so provoked on hearing this indictment, that fuming with anger, he raised his sword to kill his own brother. Seeing this, Hari, the knower of everyone's heart, asked Arjuna, "I don't see what impelled you to raise your weapon on your elder brother! The son of Dhritarashtra has been made object of time by Bhima. You came here out of concern for Yudhisthira's well-being, now you have confirmed he is ok. I don't see why anybody should be killed here. So why are you raising your weapon?"

The enraged Arjuna, hissing and breathing heavily out of uncontrolled anger towards Yudhisthira expressed, "O Keshava! I have vowed to behead anyone who claims that I should give away my *Gandiva*. O Govinda! Yudhisthira has spoken these very words in Your presence, so how can I forgive him? After all I am indebted to my pledge and must slay Yudhisthira. But You can guide me to act righteously. You know the past and present, so I will do as You order me."

Mukunda said, "Fie on you Arjuna! It looks like you have not served your superiors; hence your anger is unreasonable. The one, who knows *dharma*, will not retaliate like this. You lack wisdom and sensitivity. A person is the lowest of all humans if he does something that is right but impossible to execute or something that is possible but forbidden.

"Choosing ignorance as *dharma* is *adharma* by all means. Not to hurt any living entity is the greatest non-violence, and in My opinion, even if you lie to achieve this, it is *dharmik*. Your vow is childish and immature. Truth is the highest and most auspicious, but proper application of this principle, as practiced by saintly people, is very difficult to comprehend. If by lying, highest good is achieved than that is *dharma* and if by speaking the truth, violence is the outcome then that is the highest *adharma*. This is the principle of consequential truth. Speak only those words, which are consequential truth. Only such a person is the knower of *dharma* in essence."

To illustrate this point, Yashodanandana narrated Arjuna the story of a sage who had vowed to always speak the truth. So when a butcher came looking for a cow, which had slipped away from his knife, he spoke the truth by telling where the cow went. Thus by choosing truth over protecting the cow, he went to hell. On the other hand, one hunter shot an animal, which was a demon in its previous life. That animal, though born blind, had taken a vow of destroying all other living entities. By killing it, that hunter became the cause of relief to all and was sent to heaven, while the sage who had vowed not to lie went to hell.

Vanamali continued, "It is certainly not easy to decipher *dharma* unless one hears it from a superior personality who knows the subtle nuances of scriptures."

Hearing all this from Shyamsundar, Arjuna was deeply relieved and said, "You are everything to us. I would have suffered eternal perdition for the actions I was tempted to perform. You rescued me. Now how do I fulfill my vow, without killing Yudhisthira"

Dwarkadhish added, "O Arjuna! You have always respected your brother but to fulfill your vow, today you should address him disrespectfully as that is like killing him. Yudhisthira will consider that to be as good as death, but since he knows *dharma*, he will forgive your crime."

Arjuna acted according to Keshava's will, but felt so remorseful for the crime of criticizing his brother that he felt like giving up his life. Madhava said, "Simply some disrespectful words have made you so remorseful that you want to commit suicide. O Arjuna! Had you actually killed your brother, what would your state have been? Suicide is a condemnable crime, more severe than murder and never recommended by the scriptures. And to glorify your own self is as good as killing oneself". Arjuna promptly glorified himself, as a repentance for criticizing his brother, as self-glory is equal to giving up one's life.

But Arjuna's harsh and disrespectful words greatly pained Yudhisthira. Guilt-ridden, he said, "Certainly, my activities are deplorable. Because of me, you are all suffering! I am the lowest among our whole family. I am sinful, cowardly and vile therefore you should cut off my head. I do not respect the superiors. Let me go the forest, Bhima can be a better king." Grief-stricken, Yudhisthira began to proceed towards the forest.

Arjuna fell at the feet of his illustrious brother and earnestly begged forgiveness, saying, "My dear brother, there is nothing in my life other than to please you, this is the reality. I promise you, it is only a question of time that Karna will be killed."

Dinanatha grasped Yudhisthira's feet, saying, "O King, you are certainly aware of Arjuna's vow. On My order, to protect his vow, Arjuna insulted you. In fact, it was My fault, please forgive Me. For the sake of protecting the truth, please forgive both of us. We both fall at your feet, and take your shelter. Today Mother Earth will taste Karna's blood."

Hearing these words of Madhusudana, Yudhisthira, immediately held and raised Him, and with folded hands, spoke humbly, "O Govinda! Whatever You say is certainly right, I have broken certain rules and You have pacified me, and saved us from drowning in the ocean of misery. Today by accepting the boat of Your intelligent words, even though we were drowning, we have crossed this ocean safely. You are our only savior and Your protection is our only asset."

With a remorseful heart, Arjuna supplicated and Purushottama also consoled Yudhisthira. Arjuna broke down and fell at Yudhisthira's feet. Yudhisthira then raised and embraced him. Bathing each other with tears of love, they completely cleansed the dirt from their minds. Yudhisthira lovingly smelt Arjuna's head, speaking very affectionate words and blessed him to be victorious in the war.

This one incident reveals how Dwarkadhish protected the Pandavas in so many ways. He protected Arjuna from the sin of killing his brother and from the ghastly act of committing suicide. Mukunda saved Arjuna from not fulfilling his vow, by proposing the best possible alternative of condemning his elder brother. Hari willingly fell at the feet of Yudhisthira to protect him from abandoning his duties. He protected both the brothers by making them understand the subtle aspect of *dharma*. He certainly protected Arjuna's confidence in doing what he was supposed to do, kill the greatest warrior Karna, who was hell bent upon fighting on the side of evil, and being conscious of his evil of supporting his unscrupulous friend Duryodhana, had to perish.

chapter 21
DHARMA PREVAILS

Now it was time for the ultimate battle. The battle between victory and defeat, life and death, *dharma* and evil, ethical and corrupt, dexterity and culture, the doer and the instrument, self-glory and great cause! It was the battle between Karna and Arjuna.

Arjuna asked Achyuta if Karna could defeat him. He responded strongly, "My dear Partha, it is possible that the sun may fall, the ocean may dry up and fire may turn cold, but it is impossible for Karna to kill you. By chance, if this happens, then I shall destroy the whole universe and turn it upside down by My shoulders. I shall pulverise Karna and Shalya". On witnessing the protection from his worshipable Dinabandhu, Arjuna held the flag of Hanuman, smiled and fearlessly spoke, "O Janardhana! Karna and Shalya are manageable for me. You shall witness today that with my armour, umbrella, along with *Shakti* weapon and arrows, I shall destroy Karna and Shalya".

Very confidently and boldly Arjuna expressed, "O Govinda! When Karna is killed, You will hear these sweet words from me informing you - 'O Vrishninandana! It is very auspicious. Today You were victorious. Today You shall congratulate the mother of Subhadra and Your aunt Kunti. O Madhava! You shall wash the tears of Draupadi who has suffered so much. My dear Krishna, today You shall shower the nectarean news of Karna's death unto the heroic Yudhisthira and thus pacify him.'"

The ferocity of the war increased as it progressed and as these two warriors clashed with each other, they grew more and more

107

wrathful. Like two infuriated Himalayan elephants pitted against each other, like a mass of clouds encountering another mass, or a massive mountain encountering another, those two warriors, both showering torrents of arrows, encountered each other, their bows loudly twanging all the while, with their bow-strings and palms emitting intense sounds and the wheels of their chariots producing a deafening clatter. The fight between the two ensued for a long time.

At one point Karna picked the long and powerful shafted arrow known as *Sarpamukhastra*, which was fit enough to kill Arjuna. Karna lifted the arrow and as he was about to release it, Shalya intervened and suggested, "Do not target his neck; target his head." Being distracted, Karna spoke, "I do not change the object of my aim." Karna then shot the very powerful *Sarpamukhastra*, which made its way to Arjuna, flying through the sky.

Purushottama, noticing the arrow approaching with the speed of wind, gently pressed the chariot with His foot, getting the wheel stuck in the soil. Simultaneously the horses had bent down on their hoofs, so the arrow, which was on its course to sever Arjuna's head had to make do by striking his beautiful crown instead. Every assembled warrior appreciated the ingenious Parthasarathi.

On Arjuna being thus protected by Madhava, Karna got vexed. A snake, which was the personification of that very powerful *Sarpamukhastra*, returned to Karna and said, "You did not properly target Arjuna's head, please do so again and release your weapon. Nobody can protect Arjuna."

On being questioned by Karna, the snake revealed, "Arjuna is my enemy. He had killed my mother in the Khandava forest, therefore I am seeking revenge." Karna, who wasn't intending to take assistance of *sarpa* again, said, "I am powerful enough to vanquish Arjuna myself and do not need any assistance." On hearing Karna, the agitated snake decided to kill Arjuna on its own.

Then Murari glancing at Arjuna, said "O Kuntinandana! This snake is your enemy, you must kill him without delay." The surprised Arjuna, inquired, "Who is this snake?" Krishna replied, "In Khandavaprastha, when you were satisfying Agnideva (fire god), this snake was released by his mother, but his mother died. Since then, this snake has maintained enmity towards you and wants to kill you." Meanwhile, the snake darted across the chariot to attack but Arjuna sharply shot multiple arrows and killed the snake before it could strike. Hari immediately descended the chariot, and pulled out the wheel which he had pressed down on purpose and got Arjuna ready to fight again.

ARJUNA KILLS KARNA

At one point during the battle, Karna fell almost unconscious on the chariot; Arjuna could have seized this opportunity but being pious, refrained from doing so. Nandanandana chastised Arjuna, saying, "When the enemy is weak, that is the time to strike and destroy him."

Just at that moment, as if by providence, Karna's chariot got stuck in the mud. Karna began condemning *dharma*, "That very *dharma* which I practice and live by every moment is now abandoning me, therefore I am convinced that *dharma* does not protect."

Meanwhile, when his chariot got stuck, he beseeched Arjuna, "O Dhanurdhara! O Kunti-Kumar! Just be patient, I shall release the wheel from the earth and resume our battle. You cannot kill me by fraudulent means. One who accepts the path of immorality is a coward. You certainly don't tread that path. You are known to be the greatest of warriors. This is the time to prove it. Arjuna, those with loosened hair, those astray from the battlefield, the *brahmanas*, those who have folded their hands, those who have surrendered their weapons, those seeking mercy, and those with broken bow and arrows, should not be attacked by warriors who are followers of great vows. O Pandunandana! You are the greatest among heroes, you are virtuous, you are the knower of *dharma* and you have studied *Vedanta*. Therefore it is not befitting you to strike me when I am in such a compromised position. O Son of Pandu! I neither fear you nor Madhusudana. As an able descendent, you increase the greatness of your *kshatriya* dynasty, thus I am speaking these words. Therefore, stop, and wait for me to rise."

Here Mukunda again protected Arjuna from the weakness of heart caused by a shrewd opponent's strategy of proselytizing *dharma*, which he himself had failed to uphold on this battlefield of Kurukshetra. The all knower, Adhokshaja, had to arouse Arjuna out of his vacillating heart and teach him the real religion, *sudharma*.

He thus spoke to Karna, "O Radhanandana! It is your good fortune that you are remembering *dharma* today. It is generally seen that those who are in difficulty easily condemn their *daiva* but seldom their own bad behaviour. O Karna! At the time, when, along with Duryodhana, Dushasana, and Shakuni, you dragged Draupadi, where was your realization of *dharma*? When in the assembly of the Kurus, Yudhisthira Maharaja, who did not know how to gamble, was made to lose by foul play, where was your *dharma*? When the Pandavas had finished thirteen years of exile, and when your immorality did not allow them to get back to their kingdom, what had happened to your understanding of *dharma*? Bhima was poisoned on the advice of Shakuni and your good self, at that time where was your *dharma*? When the

110

Pandavas were about to be burnt in the Varnavata, where was your *dharma*? When Draupadi was being dragged by Dushasana and you ridiculed her, where was your *dharma*? You told Draupadi that her husbands would fall into hellish planets forever, asking her to accept somebody else as her husband, lustfully staring at her all the while, where was your *dharma* then? When you invited the Pandavas to gamble for the second time, where was your *dharma*? Where was your *dharma* while the son of Arjuna, the great Abhimanyu, was irreligiously and brutally killed?"

On being reminded by Shyamsundar of all the ruthlessness of Karna and the Kauravas, all of Arjuna's tears, pain and anger swelled up within him.

Keshava directed Arjuna to aim the *Anjulika* weapon at Karna. "As long as Karna is off his chariot, you can cut off his head," said Keshava. Following the order of the Supreme Personality, and remembering all the sinister actions of Karna and the Kauravas, Arjuna held the *Anjulika* weapon and exclaimed, "Let this great *divyastra* sever Karna's head from his body. Only if I have ever performed *tapasya*, service to my superiors, *yagya* and good deeds towards my friends, with the weapon of *satya*, let this powerful *Anjulika* cut off Karna's head."

Just as Arjuna uttered these words, the mighty weapon charged, cutting through the air and struck Karna, severing his head, which fell off to the ground. In this way, Karna, the son of Sun God, lost his life.

Arjuna, thus fulfilled the promise he had made to Yudhisthira Maharaja, giving him and the entire Kuru kingdom great pleasure, and at the same time, fulfilling and assisting the Supreme Lord Sri Krishna in establishing *dharma*. He had conquered the greatest of the warriors in this most decisive battle to make Duryodhana completely and forever hopeless of reigning over Hastinapura.

BATTLE OF BHIMA AND DURYODHANA

With the death of Karna, and then Shalya, Duryodhana became a lone fighter. Being exhausted and tired, he went to Dvaipayana *sarovara*, where he rested, reflecting upon his fate. Meanwhile, the Pandavas were frantically searching for him everywhere. Hari had taught them not to spare even the slightest trace of the enemy, lest he grows again, only to attack later.

As the Pandavas came to know of his whereabouts, Yudhisthira approached Duryodhana out of his simplicity, which could have spelt disaster for the Pandavas, saying, "Duryodhana, you choose any one of us to fight, and if you win, the kingdom will be yours."

Madhava, hearing these words from Yudhisthira rebuked him, "You fool! You have started the gambling match again, I think the sons of Kunti are not destined to rule. No one other than Bhima, and that too, only through illusion, can defeat Duryodhana." Bhima pacified Keshava and said, "I will fight him and fulfill the vow I made in the gambling assembly to break his thighs."

As Duryodhana came out to fight, ready to strike his long-standing enemy, Bhima, Arjuna inquired, "Who amongst them will win, Madhava? What is their strength and weakness?" Kamalalocana replied, "O Partha! Bhima is more powerful while Duryodhana has skills on his side. While you were all in exile, Duryodhana unfailingly practiced mace fighting with the sinister intention of killing Bhima. On the other hand, Bhima did not get to practice. Another critical factor is, someone who is about to lose his life, has nothing more to be lost, hence will fight fiercely. Only by *adharma* can Bhima bring him down."

As the combat between Bhima and Duryodhana was about to

begin, Balarama appeared on the scene, returning from his long pilgrimage. Both Bhima and Duryodhana, His students, then took His blessings and began to fight. Both warriors were determined to strike each other. They resembled moving mountains, striking thunder and torrential rain.

At one point, when Duryodhana struck Bhima, he almost became unconscious. Duryodhana thought, Bhima was preparing for a powerful attack, while he was actually in a spell of unconsciousness, hence he waited for Bhima's reaction and did not hit.

Meanwhile Arjuna again inquired about the outcome of the battle from Madhava, who reminded Arjuna to prompt Bhima to strike Duryodhana below the belt, even though according to the standards of mace fighting this was not permitted. But Bhima's vow to break Duryodhana's thighs was well known, so Bhima had to be reminded to strike there.

As Duryodhana leapt in the sky moving backwards, Arjuna struck his own thighs to remind Bhima to attack him there. Bhima, who was looking for inroads, as if awakened to reality by this reminder, eventually struck Duryodhana below the belt, and broke his thighs. Shocked, Duryodhana fell to the ground in great pain. As Duryodhana crashed, Bhima, remembering all the sins he had committed, struck his head which was adorned with the crown of Hastinapura, all the while swearing vehemently at him.

When Balarama saw that Bhima had struck Duryodhana below the belt and placed his foot on Duryodhana's head, He condemned Bhima, "Fie on you! You shouldn't have hit him below the belt, but since you are not well-versed in the injunctions of the scriptures, you have done so."

Haladhara turned furious and said, "O Muralimohan, Duryodhana was as powerful as Me. There is no one equal to him, but today, due to injustice he has been brought down. And by doing so, Bhima has offended Me too. To attack the weakness of an opponent which is against the rules of mace fighting is a great sin." Haladhara, saying this, picked up his mace to attack Bhima, who was not at all afraid of Him.

Krishna immediately came and stood between Balarama and Bhima. It was a beautiful scene, with Ghanashyam, who resembled a black mountain contrasting Balarama, who resembled a white mountain. Rohininandana was looking like the Kailash Mountain and Shyamsundar was looking like the mountain of mascara (*kajal*).

Sri Krishna attempted to placate Sankarashana saying, "My dear brother, please quell your anger. After all, the Pandavas are our relatives and friends. In their prosperity lies ours. They have taken shelter of Purushartha, their hard labour. So I know what Bhima has done. As a *kshatriya* he fulfilled his promise and therefore broke Duryodhana's thighs. In fact, Maharishi Maitreya had predicted this therefore I do not see any fault in Bhima's actions. You should not be upset, because we have a relationship with the Pandavas. My dear brother, please calm down."

Balabhadra was still not appeased. He said, "Great people have followed *dharma* very nicely but because of *artha* and *kama*, today *dharma* has been minimized. One who is too greedy is weak in his *dharma*; therefore what has been done today is not good. O Govinda! Simply because of *artha*, Bhima has destroyed *dharma*, he has perverted it and it is very strange that You are approving this!"

Hrishikesh spoke to Ananta, "My dear brother, You are known to be free from anger and a diligent adherent of *dharma*, therefore I request You to be peaceful. Please try to understand that

114

Kaliyuga has come, and remember the vows of Bhima. Bhima has simply fulfilled his pledge and freed himself from the debt of that promise. Bhima has killed the evil-minded Duryodhana. You should remember that during the battle, this very Duryodhana had ordered Karna to go behind Abhimanyu and cut off his bow and Karna obeyed. As Abhimanyu's bow was cut, he became defenceless. He would never show his back to the warriors but all these evil people struck him from behind. This Duryodhana, who has been struck by Bhima, was the most fallen amongst fallen, and the greatest transgressor among the Kurus. Everyone is aware that Bhima had taken this vow thirteen years ago. It was Duryodhana's responsibility to remember Bhima's promise and because Duryodhana was about to strike Bhima when he was in the sky and not on the ground, thus Bhima struck him. Therefore, I do not see any fault in Bhima."

As Ajitatma spoke these words, apparently sounding deceptive, Baladeva was still not pacified. He said, "It was wrong on the part of Bhima to have hit him below the belt, so in My opinion Bhima has performed great *adharma*." Thus, Baladeva was very angry. He mounted His chariot and left that place.

The Pandavas were disheartened to see this. Then Yadunatha spoke to Yudhisthira, "My dear Yudhisthira, how come, even while witnessing Bhima putting his foot on Duryodhana's head, you didn't check him?"

Yudhisthira replied, "My dear Govinda, I was not agreeable to this but what could be done? This son of Dhritarashtra had acted so deceptively and unjustly against us in so many ways. Bhima had pent up all this within his heart for many years. Empathizing with his pain, I overlooked Bhima's action. Thus, I only remember that Bhima has fulfilled his vow by killing the man who was full of *adharma* and avarice."

Kamalalochana, with great difficulty, accepted what Yudhisthira said. Then Yudhisthira prodded Bhima, "O Bhima! It is your good fortune that today your enmity towards the Kauravas is over. Now Duryodhana has fallen. In the opinion of Achyuta, you have become victorious."

KRISHNA DEFENDS THE PANDAVAS AT THE DEATH OF DURYODHANA

Duryodhana contended with Giridhari that the battle was fought unfairly. He reminded how Bhishma, Dronacharya, Bhurishrava and Karna were unscrupulously killed. Strangely, everyone including the *gandharvas* and *apsaras* accepted Duryodhana's logic.

After hearing the words of Duryodhana, the heavenly denizens were convinced that Bhishma, Drona, Karna and Bhurishrava had been killed by *adharma*.

The *gandharvas* and *apsaras* started showering flowers on him and singing beautiful songs. The *siddhas* said, "Kudos! Kudos!" Cool breeze started flowing and the sky turned beautiful.

But unfortunately they all failed to grasp the very essence and backing behind those actions of the Pandavas. Mukunda was trying to present the whole picture to Duryodhana but, being very arrogant, he wouldn't listen. He only spoke about how they were killed, but never discussed their conduct when alive. Their lives were replete with deception, erroneous assumptions and fatal vows, and they were causing so much havoc in the world! To remove this *adharma*, which had become formidable, from the land of *dharma*, was not easy.

116

Seeing the Pandavas shocked and ashamed by this insinuation, Dwarkadhish reassured them like a rumbling cloud, "O Pandavas! Duryodhana was known for his swiftness and it was a herculean task to defeat him. Similarly, Bhishma, Drona and others were invincible warriors; to kill them in a straightforward battle was not possible. Therefore, keeping the higher principle of establishing *dharma* in mind and for your ultimate benefit, I had to repeatedly trick them with illusion. If I had not done so, victory would be farfetched. Then how would you have attained the kingdom?

"Bhishma, Drona, Karna and Bhurishrava were the greatest *atirathis* of all times! Even the great controller of the universe would not have been able to conquer them in battle. Even *kala* personified, holding his weapon could not destroy Duryodhana, who never tired out. So how was it possible for all of them to be defeated? Just like the demigods had to use tricks to destroy the demons, it was justified on My part to use whatever tools we had to destroy them." By explaining thus, Janardhana pacified the affected Pandavas. Relieved, they sounded their conch shells and proceeded towards their camp.

Through this entire episode of fighting Duryodhana, Purushottama is vividly demonstrating how the world only sees and gets influenced by the present. It was true that Duryodhana was killed by unfair means, and certainly Bhima putting his foot on Duryodhana's head was foul. It was inappropriate that Bhima spoke harshly to Duryodhana, and it was righteous of Rohininandana to find very obvious faults in Bhima's actions. It was fair on the part of the *siddhas*, *gandharvas* and *apsaras* to desire a just fight between Duryodhana and Bhima.

But it was irrefutably unfair on behalf of all these people not to have considered the past, present and future scenarios and their consequences. Getting emotionally affected by somebody's death is natural but making conclusions based upon emotional outbursts is *adharmik*.

Shyamsundar never lost sight of *dharma's* influence on the past, present and future. If there was a choice between the Pandavas winning at the cost of practicing *adharma* on the battlefield as opposed to the Kauravas emerging successful, having apparently followed *dharma* on the battlefield, justice would still tilt in favour of the Pandavas. It was better that the Pandavas survived despite having performed a little *adharma* on the battlefield of Kurukshetra because being anointed with good qualities such as virtuosity, honesty, and righteousness, only they were qualified and competent to establish a *dharmik* kingdom.

Therefore, the Supreme Adideva, who had descended to this material world to establish *dharma* was not whimsical, unreasonable, illogical or cruel in His strategic actions. Rather He was utmost sensitive. Therefore, Madhusudana reinstated the Pandavas' confidence, even though the heavenly denizens and His own expansion, Balarama, apparently showed contempt towards them. This is how Dinabandhu protected the Pandavas from feeling guilty, shameful and inconsequential. Therefore, Madhava boosted their confidence, making them relevant, consistent and responsible so that they could lead the world towards *dharma* authoritatively, as the Kings of Hastinapura!

chapter 22
CHARIOT BURNT & JEWEL REMOVED

After the enormously significant victory over Duryodhana, the Pandavas returned to their base camp. Then they proceeded to visit Duryodhana's camp, which had become a painful sight. The once vibrant camp of Duryodhana had now become barren and bereft of its beauty. The chief is the heart and soul of a camp and his presence makes it spirited.

On seeing the Pandavas approaching, the surviving soldiers of Duryodhana's army were petrified. With folded hands, they requested the compassionate blessings of the Pandavas.

In a short while, Vanamali escorted the Pandavas out and told Arjuna, "O Sabyasachi! Please remove your inexhaustible quiver, bring down your *Gandiva* and get off the chariot. I shall get off only after you. This is important for your welfare." Although this spiked his curiosity, Arjuna submissively obeyed Achyuta and got down. Then Parthasarathi, leaving the reins of the horses, jumped off the chariot awarded by Agni, which had assisted Arjuna in numerous battles. As soon as Murari descended from the chariot, Hanuman disappeared from the flag.

Now, with Arjuna and Parthasarathi off, the chariot along with the reins, wheels and horses instantly burned to ashes. When the Pandavas saw this spectacle, with folded hands Arjuna affectionately inquired, "O Govinda! How is this chariot being burnt to ashes? Please explain if you feel it appropriate to do so."

Devakinandana said, "O Gudakesha! Tormentor of the enemies! This chariot had already been destroyed by divine weapons. But because of My presence on it, you did not notice it. Now that I have left the chariot and your purpose has been fulfilled, this chariot has burned down, although the *Brahmastra* had destroyed it much before." He was referring to the divine weapons released by Karna, Bhishma and Drona.

Then, approaching Yudhisthira, Sri Krishna heartily congratulated him. Janardhana then said, "O Yudhisthira, at the beginning of the battle you had urged Me saying, 'Arjuna is Your friend and brother, please protect him.' I had assured you that I would surely do so. Now that victory is yours, we see that all of you have been protected."

Hearing this, the hair on Yudhisthira's body stood on end. He said, "My dear Brajanatha, Dronacharya and Karna had released the *Brahmastra*. Who could have saved us from it? Even Indra was not competent enough to protect us. Only by Your grace, ferocious demons were destroyed. All our desires are fulfilled. In Upaplavya, Maharishi Vyasadeva had informed us, wherever there is *dharma*, there is Sri Krishna and wherever there is Sri Krishna, there is victory."

After thus glorifying Achyuta, the Pandavas collected all the wealth that belonged to the Kurus and decided to stay in their own camp. But Madhava, being very alert to protect the Pandavas, suggested that it would be better to stay off the camp. They agreed and stayed on the bank of the most pious river Aughavati instead.

ASHWATHAMA PROTECTED

As Madhava was about to leave Hastinapura after duly consoling Dhritarashtra and Gandhari, He foresaw that Ashwathama was a threat. He knew that to fulfill the desire of Duryodhana, Ashwathama had pledged to kill the Pandavas. After taking

120

blessings of Maharishi Vyasadeva, Madhava visited the Pandavas. That night, the Pandavas did not rest in their usual camp but stayed on the banks of the Aughavati River instead. That same night, the ferocious Ashwathama, empowered by the destructive energy of Lord Shiva, attacked the Pandava camp and mercilessly killed all the sons of Draupadi as well as Dhrishtadyumna, Shikhandi and many other warriors.

When this news was brought to the Pandavas by the charioteer of Dhrishtadyumna, Yudhisthira Maharaja, Draupadi and other Pandavas lamented at the profound loss. Draupadi enjoined Bhima to kill Ashwathama, but Yudhisthira Maharaja asked her, "Since he has run away to the forest, even if we kill him, how would you know for sure that we have done so?" To this, Draupadi replied saying she wanted the beautiful jewel from Ashwathama's forehead, only then she would be convinced of his due punishment. She gave the ultimatum that unless this was done she would fast-unto-death.

As Bhima was about to leave on his chariot to avenge Ashwathama for his gruesome act, Govinda informed Arjuna how dangerous Ashwathama was. He related an incident when he had received the *Brahmastra* weapon from his father. This was when the Pandavas were in exile. Upon receiving it, he had visited Krishna and said, "My dear Achyuta, please let us exchange our weapons. I will give You my *Brahmastra* and You give me Your *Sudarshana* weapon in exchange." Krishna was willing to give any weapon he wanted - His bow, *Shakti, Chakra* or mace. Ashwathama could not handle it. So Achyuta asked Ashwathama how he would use it. He said, "I wanted to use this weapon against You and become unconquerable by anyone in the world."

Krishna thus explained that Ashwathama was so dangerously unpredictable that he could do anything.

As the Pandavas approached Ashwathama, with Bhima closing in on him, the petrified Ashwathama let loose the *Brahmastra* against the Pandavas to protect his life. Seeing this, Vanamali suggested, "O Pandunandana Arjuna! This is the time to put all the knowledge you have received from your guru Dronacharya to counteract this *Brahmastra*, and protect your brothers and army."

Arjuna promptly released another *Brahmastra*. As the two *Brahmastras* were attacking each other, all the great *rishis* headed by Vyasadeva and Narada Muni arrived and asked Arjuna, "There were many great *maharathis* but they never released the *Brahmastra*, so why have you done this destructive act? How could you do this?"

Realising the calamity his action could cause, Arjuna said, "I only released it to counteract the *Brahmastra* of Ashwathama. Otherwise, he would have killed us all. But I will do as you say, as you are equal to God." Saying this, he withdrew the weapon.

However, Ashwathama did not know how to withdraw his *Brahmastra*. It could only be withdrawn by one who practices severe penances in *brahmacharya*. Arjuna had received that weapon when he was staying in guru Dronacharya's *ashram* but Ashwathama, even though unqualified had received it from his father on insistence.

Vyasadeva chastised Ashwathama, and then told him, "If you want the Pandavas to be pacified, then give them the jewel from your forehead." Though initially unwilling, eventually he realized that it was the only way he could survive.

Meanwhile, as Ashwathama didn't know how to withdraw the *Brahmastra*, he told Vyasadeva, "I am going to release this weapon and destroy the last remaining member in the lineage of the Pandavas and nobody can stop this." Vyasadeva said, "Do whatever you want to. Drop that weapon on the womb of Uttara." Thus, Ashwathama targeted the *Brahmastra* at Uttara's womb.

In a way, Hrishikesh was very pleased by this. He then told Ashwathama, "When Arjuna's son Abhimanyu and his wife Uttara were staying in the kingdom of Virata, once a *brahmana* had foretold that when the dynasty of the Kauravas would be destroyed, Uttara would beget a nice son who would be named Parikshit. He will take the lineage of the Pandavas forward."

Hearing this, Ashwathama furiously said, "I know You always favour the Pandavas but my weapon will not go in vain and Parikshit will certainly be killed. Nobody can protect him."

Damodara replied, "Ashwathama, certainly the *Brahmastra* never misses its target. The child in Uttara's womb will be killed but, nevertheless, I assure you that he will have a long life. He will practice *brahmacharya*, and ardently follow *Vedic* scriptures. Kripacharya will offer him all kinds of weapons. He will be well-situated in the great *kshatriya dharma*. Being the king of the entire planet Earth, Maharaja Parikshit will rule for sixty years.

"But you will surely face the reaction for being a murderer of children. For three thousand years, you will roam around the earthly planet. You will never be able to stay in one place. Nobody will talk to you and your body will stink. It will ooze blood and pus, you will have to stay in the most remote areas and all kinds of diseases will afflict you."

Hari was very confident being the Supreme Lord Himself. In this way He promised the Pandavas that their protection was guaranteed. How Ameyatma protected Parikshit has been described further in this book.

After receiving the jewel, the Pandavas brought it back and offered it to Draupadi, and thus Ashwathama was protected, although he was to now face his fate for the next three thousand years.

chapter 23
THE OLD COUPLE'S ATTEMPT FOILED

After cursing Ashwathama, the Pandavas lamented the death of their sons and Yudhisthira Maharaja asked Mukunda, "How is it that Dhrishtadyumna and other Pandavas who were very powerful could be killed by Ashwathama? What was the force that made Ashwathama kill the younger Pandavas, Shikhandi and Dristadhyumna?"

Shridhara explained to Yudhisthira, "Ashwathama was empowered by the destructive energy of Lord Shiva. Even Indra would have found it difficult to stop him and therefore this was ordained".

The Pandavas then went to meet Dhritarashtra. As they approached Dhritarashtra, offering their obeisances, they saw that he was in great pain of separation from his departed sons. Dhritarashtra embraced Yudhisthira Maharaja but his mind was not at peace.

There was great hostility in his heart towards Bhima. The burning embers of his indignation towards Bhima got further inflamed by the winds of lamentation he felt from the colossal loss of Duryodhana. It was as if he wanted to burn Bhima to ashes.

Understanding Dhritarashtra's heart, Achyuta forbade Bhima from approaching Dhritarashtra to embrace him. Instead He pushed an iron statue that exactly resembled Bhima, in front of Dhritarashtra. Knowing well what would happen, Padmanabha had already pre-empted this and arranged for such a statue. As Dhritarashtra came closer, identifying that statue to be Bhima,

125

he hugged it so intensely that the solid iron statue was crushed to pieces.

Bhima was astounded to see this. Dhritarashtra, thinking he had killed Bhima, feigned a cry, "O Bhima! O Bhima! What have I done?" But Giridhari told Dhritarashtra, "Do not lament, you did not kill Bhima. You have pulverised a statue instead. But your anger could have killed Bhima. Who could release himself from the clutches of your indomitably powerful arms? Today I have saved Bhima. But what is the use of attempting to kill him? Even if you succeed at it, your dead sons will never be revived because they have already attained their destination according to their actions."

In this way, Madanmohan, because of His presence of mind, was able to protect Bhima, who was about to be crushed by Dhritarashtra.

GANDHARI'S CURSE

After this meet with Dhritarashtra, the Pandavas decided to approach Gandhari. Meanwhile Vyasadeva, the literary incarnation of Sri Krishna, realizing that Gandhari's spite would impel her to curse the Pandavas, rushed to her.

Consoling her, he spoke pacifying words, "Everyday Duryodhana would come to seek your blessings for victory and you, being such an extraordinarily pious and powerful lady, would always tell Duryodhana that wherever there is *dharma*, certainly there is victory". Therefore, Vyasadeva urged Gandhari, "You have always been devout, forgiving and an upholder of *dharma*. A lady of your stature should certainly forgive the Pandavas as neither were they at fault nor did they ever harness ill-feelings towards anyone." Thus placating her, Vyasadeva convinced Gandhari not to curse the Pandavas. When the Pandavas appeared in

Gandhari's presence, she asked them a few questions but eventually blessed them all.

But when Vyasadeva, with a divine vision, showed Gandhari the entire battlefield of Kurukshetra, with many great personalities who fought the war lying dead on the battlefield, she couldn't handle it.

Out of great anger and pain, Gandhari cursed Yadunatha and the Yadavas that within thirty-six years their entire dynasty would be destroyed in a fratricidal fight.

Of course, can anyone possibly curse the Lord? But the Lord being very compassionate empathized with Gandhari's pain and smilingly spoke to her when she cursed Him. Lord Dwarkanatha said, "I certainly knew what would happen - no one could destroy the Yadu dynasty but you have made this possible by your curse. Therefore your prediction will certainly come to pass."

The Pandavas were very dejected to hear this. Actually, Gandhari cursing Devakinandana was not very significant. However, it is noteworthy that after doing so, she had used up all her power and chastity to curse the Yadavas, which was a relief for Purushottama since this meant that Gandhari no longer had the potency to curse the Pandavas. Thus the Pandavas were completely protected. Gandhari's curse was a medium for Laxmipati to wind up His Yadu dynasty from this world and take them all back to His original abode of Vaikuntha.

BHISHMADEVA'S MEDITATION

After coming back from the palace of Dhritarashtra and Gandhari, Yudhisthira Maharaja became very despondent. He was taking all the responsibility for the war. While his coronation was soon approaching, Yudhisthira was so crestfallen that he insisted on renouncing and going to the forest as a *sannyasi* or *vanaprastha*. All the Pandavas along with Draupadi tried convincing Yudhisthira of the importance of ruling the kingdom and always upholding *dharma*. Eventually Vyasadeva assured him that Duryodhana was responsible for this war, not him. Finally, being convinced, Yudhisthira Maharaja took over the kingship and was coroneted.

One day, Yudhisthira Maharaja was glorifying Govinda, "My dear Lord, because Buddhidevi, intelligence personified, has taken Your shelter, it is by that intelligence that we have acquired our kingdom. You are the shelter for the entire world, and You are the source of all valour in this world. It is only Your compassion that has made us victorious in the war, while keeping our *dharma* intact."

Madhava did not respond to Yudhisthira Maharaja as he was in deep meditation. Yudhisthira Maharaja curiously asked Yogeshwara, "Who are You meditating upon? It is very surprising. As far as I understand, all the worlds are doing well and Your consciousness is all pervading and therefore omniscient about everything that is happening above and below. My dear Lord, who is it that You are meditating upon? Your hair is standing on end and Your mind is in *samadhi*.

"You have become inert like a stone. Just like an unwavering lamp in a windless environment, Your mind is absolutely still. If You consider me qualified, please explain the object of Your meditation. You alone are the cause of all causes including creation, maintenance and destruction of this universe and countless other universes. I have come to Your shelter, I am Your devotee. I offer my respects at Your lotus feet. O fountainhead of *dharma*! Kindly explain to me why You are meditating?"

As Yudhisthira Maharaja raised this question, Yogeshwara, smiling very sweetly, spoke, "My dear King Yudhisthira, I am meditating on the lion amongst humans – Bhishmadeva. Like a lamp exhausting its oil, he is about to quit his body and I am meditating upon him. He has performed unlimited super-human tasks in his lifetime and therefore I would like to go and see him".

As Yadunatha was very intensely meditating on Bhishmadeva, he too was meditating upon Him. Mukunda instructed the Pandavas to accompany Him and asked Satyaki to prepare His chariot, and went to the place where Bhishma was lying on the bed of arrows, awaiting his departure. Bhishma was waiting for the sun to come into *Uttarayana*, but more importantly, he was waiting for the King of demigods – Adideva to arrive so that he could quit his body in His presence, after receiving His mercy.

Although during the battle, Yadunatha certainly chastised His pure devotee Bhishmadeva for standing against *dharma*, He did not give up on him at the time of his demise from this plane. Instead, remembering him, He came to bestow His unlimited mercy at the time of his departure of His own will.

chapter 24

BHISHMADEVA'S DEPARTURE & PARIKSHIT'S APPEARANCE

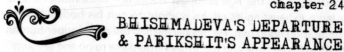

After Yudhisthira Maharaja was coroneted, Dwarkadhish went to see Bhishmadeva and requested him to instruct Yudhisthira, who was lamenting on the massacre. Bhishmadeva said, "My dear Lord, what can I speak? You are the guru and I am the student. It is not right on my part to speak in front of You."

Hrishikesh said, "No! You should speak. You have led a selfless life and are very knowledgeable." Bhishmadeva declined on the grounds of being severely wounded, suffering boundless pain due to the arrows that had pierced his body and his tongue having become rigid due to exhaustion.

But Madanmohan, nevertheless, infused Bhishmadeva with the power, strength and inspiration to speak. Yudhisthira Maharaja asked why He chose not to speak Himself. Shyamsundar explained that He could have spoken and everyone would have so expected, since he was the knower of all knowledge.

But instead He desired to immortalize Bhishmadeva, for as long as the creation would exist, through his instructions, which would be remembered and applied by people in their lives. Moreover, the benefit of hearing Bhishmadeva speak would be the same.

In this way, Vanamali inspired Bhishmadeva to speak. Bhishmadeva, after glorifying Yashodanandana with great eagerness, began speaking to Yudhisthira for many days. He spoke about the different aspects of *dharma*, including the *Vishnu Sahastranama*.

DEATH OF BHISHMADEVA

After hearing Bhishmadeva speak on all aspects of *dharma*, Yudhisthira Maharaja was freed from all illusions, and accepted his request along with that of Devakinandana, Vyasadeva and other seniors to whole-heartedly accept the throne of Hastinapura. Thereafter Yudhisthira pacified the families of the slain warriors and recalled that the time for Bhishmadeva's departure was soon approaching. Then, along with all the family members including Dhritarashtra, Yudhisthira arrived where the great Bhishmadeva was lying on the battlefield of Kurukshetra.

As Yudhisthira Maharaja greeted his great-grandfather, Bhishmadeva, he requested him to accept service from his lowly self. Bhishmadeva then began speaking. He consoled Dhritarashtra but convinced him about Duryodhana's duplicity and reminded him of Vyasadeva's words - how Duryodhana would be the cause of the war. Bhishmadeva also said, "I tried to convince Duryodhana explaining that 'Wherever there is Ajita, there is *dharma* and wherever there is *dharma*, there is victory. Therefore my dear Duryodhana please take the assistance of Sri Krishna and be partners with the Pandavas. This is the greatest opportunity for you.' Despite my many supplications, Duryodhana never relented and therefore was vanquished by the power of time."

Bhishmadeva then glorified Vrajendranandana, "O My dear Krishna! O Devadeveshwara! I offer my obeisance unto You. O Lord Narayana! You are Vasudeva! You are Hiranayatma! Purusha! Savita! Virata! And You are the source of all living entities! You are *Paramatma*! All the demi-gods and demons fall at Your lotus feet! You have measured the entire cosmos with Your three steps as Vamanadeva! O Kamalalochana! The greatest of personalities, the personification of Vaikuntha, You are the cause of my

131

deliverance. O Madanmohan! You are the shelter of everyone, I request You to continue to protect Your great devotees. O my dear Adi, I know that You are the oldest of the personalities, Lord Narayana. You are Nara's partner, living in Badrikashrama. The great Devarshi Narada and Vyasadeva had told me that Arjuna and Krishna are *sakhas*, Nara and Narayana but they have come to this world in a human form."

Seeking consent from the Supreme Personality of Godhead, Bhishmadeva asked, "O my Lord! Now please give me permission so that I can quit this body and go back to the land beyond this world."

As Bhishmadeva spoke the glories of Shyamsundar offering Him prayers, the Lord spoke, "O protector of Prithvi! The great Bhishmadeva, I give you permission to go back to the place where you came from, to the land of Vasus. In your life, you have not sinned even a bit, you are like Markandeya *rishi*. Therefore, *mrityu* or personification of death stands as a servant at your disposal."

After Vanamali spoke these words, Bhishmadeva addressed everyone including Dhritarashtra, "I am about to leave my body, and all of you give me permission. You all try to practice *dharma* and truthfulness, because truthfulness is the highest order." He also advised everyone, "Please be sensitive to each other, control your mind and senses and be devoted to the *brahmanas* and those who practice *dharma*." After embracing his relatives, Bhishmadeva spoke, "My dear Yudhisthira, please take care of the people, especially the learned, great teachers and the *rishis*".

Bhishmadeva then withdrew all his senses from external consciousness and by his *yogic* powers gradually began to bring his *prana* to the *brahma-randhra* by blocking other places where *prana* was circulating. As he was doing this, everyone became astonished to see that all the arrows, which Arjuna had pierced his body with, slowly began to fall off and the lacerations all over his body started getting covered and healed. Eventually, the illustrious Bhishmadeva, cracking the *brahma-randhra* while being fully absorbed in his *Ishtadeva* Dwarkadhish, ascended to the higher realm, causing his life and his departure to be eternally celebrated.

SAVING YUDHISTHIRA THROUGH THE KAMA GITA

After the departure of Bhishmadeva, Yudhisthira Maharaja returned to Hastinapura and started ruling the kingdom but time and again, he would despair over the death of hundreds and millions of soldiers on the battle of Kurukshetra. Yudhisthira Maharaja's good qualities became the cause of his perennial despondency. He couldn't bear the thought that he was responsible for so many deaths. Mukunda, Vyasadeva and Dhritarashtra tried alleviating his pain in different ways but to no avail. Finally Mukunda suggested that Yudhisthira perform an *Ashwamedha yagya* so that he may be engaged in the activities of proper governance.

Achyuta also expounded the *Kama Gita* for the benefit of Yudhisthira. The essence of *Kama Gita* is surrender of 'mamakara', meaning the conception of 'I, me and mine'.

Purushottama elucidated in various ways, explaining that as long as any ruler is free from false ego, he does not commit acts of a*nartha*. On the other hand, even if a renunciant sustaining on nuts and roots in the forest gets attached to his lifestyle, he is no better than a materialist.

Yogeshwara told Yudhisthira that only through *yoga* and *vairagya* can one uproot this attachment; otherwise the all powerful 'kama' becomes our second nature. One may have been able to

133

overcome *kama* but if he maintains attachment and pride about how it was overcome, then the 'doer' mentality will make *kama* creep in again.

Padmanabha quoted *kama* personified, who says, "I appear in the *chitta* of one who performs lots of sacrifices and charity in an attempt to eliminate me. I sprout in the mind of those who are trying to eradicate me by studying *Vedas* and *Vedanta*. Those who are trying to destroy me by their determination and truthfulness, I infect them in such a way that they cannot even identify my presence. I enter the austerities of those who are performing great *vratas* or *tapasya*." In this way, *kama* is omnipresent. Hence, the best way to overcome *kama* is to perform one's prescribed duty without being attached.

Mukunda thus pacified Yudhisthira Maharaja by imparting this knowledge of *Kama Gita* to him. Without His intervention, Yudhisthira would have left for the forest, renouncing the kingdom and the world, putting Hastinapura in a very challenging situation. But with Mukunda's assistance, the great Yudhisthira Maharaja, though initially reluctant due to his boundless sensitivity, was able to successfully rule Hastinapura as per the tenets of *Nishkama Karma Yoga* – neither becoming attached to *karma* nor becoming detached to the extent of being irresponsible. This is how Achyuta repeatedly protected Yudhisthira Maharaja from vacillating between *vairagya* and kingly responsibility.

PLEADING FOR PARIKSHIT MAHARAJA

Yadunatha had returned to Hastinapura from Dwarka when Yudhisthira Maharaja was performing the *Ashvamedha Yagya*. Meanwhile, everyone was joyous that a baby was born to Uttara but on seeing that it was dead they were extremely disheartened. They were lamenting deeply as the baby was the only hope for the continuation of the Kuru legacy, since all the sons of Draupadi and Subhadra had already been killed.

When Dwarkadhish came to know that the Pandavas had lost their last heir, He hastily came to the inner chambers of the queens, accompanied by Satyaki. When Kunti saw Him, she cried out, "Krishna! Krishna!" Draupadi, Subhadra and other women were grief-stricken and wailing. When He came closer, Kunti beseeched, "My dear Lord! O Devakinandana! Your mother has been greatly glorified because she delivered You, now You are the source of our shelter. It is Your responsibility to protect our family. O My Lord! Ashwathama's weapon has killed the son of Your nephew, Abhimanyu. Please grant him life."

Kunti implored Him, "O Govinda! When Ashwathama had released this *Brahmastra*, You had vowed to bring Abhimanyu and Uttara's son back to life. Now Uttara's son has died in the womb itself, so please bestow Your mercy upon him. O Madhava! You protected Subhadra, Draupadi, Uttara and me. Oh Lord! With Your unlimited potencies, You saved Yudhisthira, Arjuna, Bhima, Nakula and Sahadeva. Now please be kind and merciful by saving this child too. Our lives will be perpetuated through this child, who will carry our ancestors' legacy forward. Please perform the auspicious activity of bringing this child back to life, thereby pleasing Your beloved Abhimanyu as well."

As Kunti was pleading thus, Sri Krishna was pacifying everyone. Then Subhadra appealed, "O dear brother! O Kamalalochana! Just see what is happening with Your bosom friend Arjuna's children. Uttara's son was to be born at the death of the Kauravas, but he himself is dead. To kill Bhima, Drona's son Ashwathama, released *Brahmastra*, which then attacked Uttara's womb. My dear Lord, now I neither have my son Abhimanyu, nor my grandson, who came out of the womb dead. What will Yudhisthira Maharaja do when he hears of this? How will Bhima feel? What will Nakula and Sahadeva think? Drona's son has ruined everything for the Pandavas."

Subhadra continued, "O Dwarkanatha, You know that Abhimanyu was very dear to the five Pandavas. What will the Pandavas do after being defeated by the powerful *astra* of Ashwathama? I fall at Your lotus feet, I want to please You. My sister Draupadi is also falling at Your feet, please protect her. When Ashwathama was trying to destroy the embryo in Uttara's womb, the only heir of the Pandavas, You had told him with great anger, "O Brahmabandhu! O Naradhama! I will never allow your desire to be fulfilled. Arjuna's grandson will certainly live." Purushottama, please fulfill Your pledge and let him be alive by Your grace!"

PARIKSHIT PROTECTED

As Subhadra was thus urging with great emotion, Dinabandhu, saw Uttara's painful condition. Then Amala Krishna, who is pure hearted and never minimized in His position, spoke, "My dear Uttara, I never lie and this is My vow. It will never go in vain. All those who are embodied will get to see how I revive this child. I have never spoken a lie, either gravely or jokingly. I have never shown My back on the battlefield. Back by this strength, I will raise Abhimanyu's son from the dead. If *dharma* and *brahmanas* are very dear to Me, O dead son of Abhimanyu, please come back. If I have never opposed Arjuna, backed by this truth, let this child come to life. If there is truthfulness and if there is continuous *dharma*, let this son of Abhimanyu come back. I have killed Kamsa and Keshi in accordance with *dharma* and on the strength of this truth let this child be born!"

As Kamsahari spoke thus, slowly the child's limbs starting moving. As Keshidamana pacified the *Brahmastra*, the inner chamber of the Pandavas started glowing. All the demons which had come to kill the child fled. A voice from the sky said, "Keshava, Keshava, All glories to You!" The *Brahmastra* returned to Brahmaloka. Thus, the child which had died in the womb was revived by Ameyatma.

As the son of Uttara and Abhimanyu started moving his limbs, all the women became overjoyed. The assembled ladies started chanting auspicious *mantras* with the help of *brahmanas*, and they all began glorifying Shyamsundar. In the meanwhile, all the *mallas*, *nattas*, *jyotishis* and *vandis*, the deliverers of auspicious news, started glorifying the Kuruvansha as well as Giridhari. Taking her baby, Uttara came to Sri Krishna and offered her obeisance. Giridhari became very pleased and showered gifts for the baby. All the Yadus also gave multitudes of gifts.

Then Achyuta, who always speaks the truth, named the child. "This grandchild of the Pandavas, the son of Abhimanyu, has been born in this world at a time when the entire family of the Kurus has been destroyed, '*pariksheena*'. He is the survivor of this family. Therefore, his name will be Parikshit."

In this way, Govinda protected the pious Pandavas and also their legacy so as to ensure sustained and continuous growth and prosperity of the great dynasty of the Pandavas.

EPILOGUE

THE DEPARTURE

Pandavas ruled their kingdom for more than thirty-six years, under the guidance of Devakinandana, and their teacher Dhaumya and *kula-guru*, Kripacharya. With the passage of time, they started to prepare for their final destination.

No *Itihasa*, or *Puranas* would ever conclude a story with the cliched 'happily ever after', because that is opposed to the very definition of this material world. When Sri Krishna and Sri Rama advent in a human form, one of the major lessons they teach us is how to depart from this world. They graphically illustrate this through their pastimes or *lilas* on the earthly plane.

Damodara was winding up his human-like pastimes, in accordance with the laws of this world. He wished to demonstrate how everything in this world comes with limitations. Hence the pastimes of the Lord's appearance and disappearance from this world are as human in nature as possible just to illustrate that nothing in this world is permanent. This is His magnanimity.

Thus Yadunatha devised the fratricidal war amongst the Yadavas, finishing the Yadu clan and eventually, Dwarka was submerged. Daruka requested Arjuna to take the surviving members of Devakinandana's family to Indraprastha, and eventually install His great grandson, Vajranabha as the king of Mathura.

As Arjuna was proceeding towards Indraprastha, he was defeated in fighting by ordinary cowherd infidels. This did not surprise him. It simply reconfirmed his conviction that all his valour and heroism was a gift of Shyamsundar. It had played its role in establishing the kingdom of *dharma* and it was no more required. Now, he had to follow in Madhava's footsteps by departing from this world.

When Arjuna returned to Indraprastha, observing his countenance, Yudhisthira could guess the worst eventuality had occurred. He feared hearing the most distressful news of Gopinatha's departure from this world and apprehensively he inquired about it. Sri Arjuna, with great agony, feeling intense separation from his most dear friend Sri Hari, narrated the entire event of the fratricidal war and the eventual departure of Sri Krishna and Sri Balarama, demonstrating Their amazing detachment for this world.

Afflicted and grief-stricken, the Pandavas decided to depart from this world too. They had already trained their grandson Parikshit, who was competent and devoted to the cause of *dharma* to take over the reins of Hastinapura.

The final destination of the Pandavas was towards the *uttara* (North) direction, which symbolizes going to higher realms of reality, beyond the mundane. They had become detached, even from each other – a natural consequence of attainment of complete wisdom. As they walked deep into the Himalayas, one after another, they began to quit their mortal frame. But the remaining members would simply proceed, not because they were inhuman, rather they were practicing the highest form of renunciation, the ultimate stage in evolution of the embodied.

Srimad Bhagavatam explains how eventually crossing all barriers, including heaven and hell, the Pandavas attained the realm of Vaikuntha, the land of limitlessness, where there is boundless service to their dear Lord and master Laxmipati. These facts are not mentioned in the *Mahabharata*.

The Pandavas were completely enamoured by Vrajendranandana, who walked them through such a journey of life, that it was a life worth living.

As typified by Madanmohan, no particular quality could be designated to Him. He had the serenity of Buddha, but He was beyond it. He had the compassion of Christ, but He was beyond it. He had the naughtiness of a teenager, but He was never conditioned or limited to it. Purushottama had the power of the greatest philosopher, but He never identified with it.

Gita, the immortal song, appeared from Sri Krishna's compassionate heart to pacify the afflicted Arjuna. Nandakumar was a kingmaker, but He never micro-managed or controlled them. Once the Pandavas started ruling, He never intervened unasked. Dinabandhu epitomized selfless service by serving His dear devotees, the Pandavas, in so many ways, but it was difficult to pin point. This quality is a characteristic of Sri Krishna - He was not bound to any qualities, rather He used all the qualities with detachment to establish the kingdom of *dharma*, and more importantly, to capture the hearts of His devotees. Imbuing His devotees' hearts with this fascination and unlimited *prema* is the establishment of the essence of all *dharmas*.

Parikshit had heard about Mukunda's divine nature from his superiors. He had heard that out of His causeless mercy, Sri Krishna, the very Vishnu who is universally obeyed by all, rendered all kinds of services to the easily impressionable sons of Pandu, by accepting posts ranging from charioteer to president to messenger to friend to night watchman and the likes, according to the will of the Pandavas, obeying them like a servant and offering obeisances like one younger in age. When he heard this, Maharaja Parikshit became overwhelmed with devotion to the lotus feet of the Lord.

Dwarkadhish is fascinating to one and all. Diving deep into His life and teachings will inundate us so much that we will perennially drown ourselves in the ocean of devotion.

Like the Pandavas, many such unalloyed devotees of Lord Krishna experienced such fascinating reciprocations from Him. This was simply a tiny drop from the ocean of His compassionate mercy towards the Pandavas from the Vyasa's *Mahabharata*.

Relishing such interaction between Dwarkadhish, and His devotees, through the sublime process of chanting and hearing the glories of the Madangopala's name, form, qualities and pastimes, constitutes the highest perfection of human existence.

AUTHOR'S PROFILE

Govinda das, an avid exponent of *Mahabharata* and *Ramayana*, has an experience of over 25 years in *Vedic* education & counseling and travels extensively all over the world sharing his reflective knowledge and wisdom. Whether counseling children, guiding families or mentoring corporate and social leaders, his profound insights are always practical, comprehensible and relevant to all cross sections.

His intellectually stimulating and analytical writing blended with the softness of his devotion strikes an appealing balance, urging his readers to be awake, alert and to make informed choices based on logically driven lessons from the scriptures.

He possesses an incessant zeal to build a bridge between the ideal and real world with a life centered around *dharmik* wisdom. His writing stems from the need to make ancient epics relevant to modern times, such that life becomes satisfying and fulfilling, driven by values and ethics expected of humanity.